"Having worked with Barry Stagn[er] [...] trust his analysis of events and his theological explanations of the issues unfolding today. I have shared platforms with him numerous times and have seen that remnant believers also trust his perception of the complicated scenarios playing out now. None of us asked to be born in the generation of the time of the signs, but I am confident that Barry will help us navigate our way and enable us to understand this time better than many teachers today."

—**Jan Markell**, founder/director, Olive Tree Ministries

"I will say what everyone is sensing: These are dynamic days, and the world seems to be preparing itself for some momentous event, whether people realize it or not. For many, trying to make sense of all that's happening has become a daunting task as everything around us is being fast-forwarded toward chaos. However, we need not despair; God's Word stands firm. *The Time of the Signs* is truly an appropriate description of the age in which we live. My friend Barry Stagner has captured well the sequence in which events will unfold as the world continues to unravel. He also reminds us in these perilous times of the glorious future that awaits us. I believe you will be encouraged and informed by reading *The Time of the Signs*."

—**Jack Hibbs**, pastor; president, Real Life Network

"The Bible is an amazing book of prophecy. In *The Time of the Signs*, Barry Stagner provides us with excellent insights in order to navigate us through the prophetic narrative. This book inspires me to keep looking expectantly for the return of Jesus. Maranatha!"

—**John Randall**, pastor,
Calvary South OC in San Clemente, CA

"Written in an accessible, practical, insightful style, this book will fill your mind with compelling truths about the signs we see proliferating all around us, signaling the soon coming of Christ. It will also stir your heart with a sense of urgency to live and serve faithfully as you wait for the rapture."

—**Dr. Mark Hitchcock**, senior pastor, Faith Bible Church, Edmond, OK;
Research Professor of Bible Exposition, Dallas Theological Seminary

THE TIME OF THE SIGNS

BARRY STAGNER

HARVEST PROPHECY
AN IMPRINT OF HARVEST HOUSE PUBLISHERS

Unless otherwise indicated, all Scripture verses are taken from the New King James Version®. Copyright © 1982 by Thomas Nelson. Used by permission. All rights reserved.

Verses marked KJV are taken from the King James Version of the Bible.

Cover design by Brock Book Design Co., Charles Brock

Cover images © Sergey Nivens / Adobe Stock

Interior design by KUHN Design Group

Map on page 164 © Harvest House Publishers

For bulk, special sales, or ministry purchases, please call 1-800-547-8979.
Email: Customerservice@hhpbooks.com

This logo is a federally registered trademark of the Hawkins Children's LLC. Harvest House Publishers, Inc., is the exclusive licensee of this trademark.

The Time of the Signs
Copyright © 2023 by Barry Stagner
Published by Harvest House Publishers
Eugene, Oregon 97408
www.harvesthousepublishers.com

ISBN 978-0-7369-8761-5 (pbk)
ISBN 978-0-7369-8762-2 (eBook)

Library of Congress Control Number: 2023938676

Printed in the United States of America

23 24 25 26 27 28 29 30 31 / BP / 10 9 8 7 6 5 4 3 2 1

Tanner, Ava, Ellie, Claire
I love being your Papa

ACKNOWLEDGMENTS

First and above all, I thank the Lord for His great love for us, His mercy and grace toward us, and for giving us His infallible Word.

Second, I am thankful for the amazing people God has brought into my life, including my wonderful family, who rode the roller coaster with me when God was working out His plan and purposes for my life and calling. I am also thankful for my church family and the awesome pastors at Calvary Central Orange County, who constantly go the extra mile so I can do what God has called me to do.

Also, I want to give a special thanks to my dear friend, brother, and co-laborer Amir Tsarfati for all the miles, hours, venues, and laughs we have shared as we've sought to reach the world with the gospel. I am grateful for your friendship and faithfulness, and your dedication to God's Word.

I also would like to thank the team at Harvest House Publishers for opening the door for me to publish this book. It is an honor and a blessing to work with the amazing people who made this happen.

I have been crucified with Christ; it is no longer
I who live, but Christ lives in me; and the life which
I now live in the flesh I live by faith in the Son of
God, who loved me and gave Himself for me.

GALATIANS 2:20

CONTENTS

FOREWORD

For years, I have taught, traveled, and toured with Barry Stagner. He is a dear friend, and I admire him greatly for his commitment to clear, Bible-based teaching free of sensationalism. His love for God's truth and his ability to help people understand and apply it has been a blessing to many.

Barry's book *The Time of the Signs* lays out, in a very skillful and readable way, the most important indicators that the end times are upon us. This is a significant work that will warn the unbeliever and bring comfort to the believer. What's remarkable is how frequently Scripture speaks about what is to come, and in this volume, Barry presents an informative and easy-to-remember chronology of how the end times will unfold. Along the way, he addresses common misperceptions people have about Bible prophecy, bringing much-needed clarity on key issues.

The Time of the Signs will provide you with a fascinating overview of all that God has planned for the future. I highly recommend reading it.

—Amir Tsarfati

A TIME LINE OF THE LAST DAYS

While there may be much room for debate concerning certain specifics regarding the subject of eschatology, the question of whether we are in the last days is not among them, as seen in the following passages:

> Peter, standing up with the eleven, raised his voice and said to them, "Men of Judea and all who dwell in Jerusalem, let this be known to you, and heed my words. For these are not drunk, as you suppose, since it is only the third hour of the day. But this is what was spoken by the prophet Joel: 'And it shall come to pass in the last days, says God, that I will pour out of My Spirit on all flesh; your sons and your daughters shall prophesy, your young men shall see visions, your old men shall dream dreams.'"
>
> ACTS 2:14-17

God, who at various times and in various ways spoke in time past to the fathers by the prophets, has in these last

days spoken to us by His Son, whom He has appointed
heir of all things, through whom also He made the worlds.

HEBREWS 1:1-2

The coming of the Son of God into the world and the birth of the
church are both indications that we are in the last days, according to
Scripture. To debate the issue is to deny God's Word. We must also
recognize that the phrase "last days" carries with it a meaning outside the coming of Jesus and the beginning of the church age. For our
purposes, the phrase "last days" will refer to what we could call the
"final days" or "closing days" of the church age and the ushering in
of the seventieth week of Daniel or, the tribulation, which will conclude with the second coming of Jesus Christ to the earth.

With that in mind, we can set the course for understanding the
subjects we will discuss and how they relate to our proximity to the
tribulation and second coming of Christ without breaching the slip-
pery slope of claiming knowledge of the day and hour of the Lord's
return for His church.

My desire in writing *The Time of the Signs* is not to introduce
every possible interpretation of prophecy held by reputable scholars, but to simply present a time line of how the events of the
last days could possibly—and in my mind, are likely to—unfold
according to Scripture. One point to keep in mind in the course
of attempting this feat is to remember that the surest form of prophetic interpretation is fulfillment. What I mean is this: For us as
fallible humans, hindsight is a better lens to look through than
foresight. The Bible has given us a great many details concerning
the last days, and apart from the Messiah Himself, it is the dominant topic of Scripture. Yet the order of some events is a subject
of much debate. My hope is to offer insight and reasonable biblical substantiation for the chronology of last-days events as shared
in this book.

The Bible has given us a great many details
concerning the last days, and apart from the
Messiah Himself, it is the dominant topic of Scripture.

It's vital for us to remember that when Bible-believing Christians differ on their eschatological interpretation of certain passages, no one's salvation is at risk. We are saved by grace through faith, not by our position on the timing of the rapture, or whether we believe the fig tree represents Israel or not, or who or what Babylon represents in Revelation.

The one caveat to this is that there are some teachings and beliefs that are strongly unbiblical regarding the last-days scenario and we are not to simply accept contrary views for the sake of unity and peace. There are certain teachings in replacement theology that we must categorically reject for multiple reasons. The primary reason is that if modern Israel is not biblical Israel, then who goes through the seventieth week of Daniel? The church. That being said, there is an apologetic element to this book. For example, doctrines like the rapture of the church will be defended scripturally, and the nations of the Ezekiel war will be identified through clear biblical and historical examination.

Few subjects have stirred up more debate and division within the church, and we would do well to heed the words that Dr. Walter Martin often repeated on his radio program, *Bible Answer Man*: "We need to agree to disagree agreeably." We should do this on all matters where the integrity of Scripture is not being challenged but interpretations vary.

Peter, Andrew, James, and John were privy to an exclusive preview of the end of things as we know them when they asked Jesus, on the Mount of Olives, about the signs of His return.

Now as He sat on the Mount of Olives, the disciples came to Him privately, saying, "Tell us, when will these things be? And what will be the sign of Your coming, and of the end of the age?"

MATTHEW 24:3

Jesus' answer is known as the Olivet Discourse and is the longest response to any question ever asked of Him. His answer, in short: It will be The Time of the Signs. A time of wars and rumors of wars, ethnic tensions, famines, disease, and geological and atmospheric anomalies, all of which will suddenly increase in frequency like labor pains.

I believe we are living in those times! We will not be making our way through a bunch of data and statistics in *The Time of the Signs*. Rather, we will examine the Scriptures and look to the times in which we live to see how far downstream we've gone and how close we are to the next transition on God's prophetic timetable. Some of the things we will consider are history that was once prophetic and has been fulfilled, at least in part, in recent history. We will talk more about this in chapter 4, but I believe there is a compact period of time in which all these things will take place prior to the millennium. The time frame will be a single generation. Are we in that generation? Can we even know if we are that generation? These are some of the questions we will try to answer along the way.

May the Lord bless you as you read along. And remember: If you see a point you disagree with, that's okay. There are some aspects of Bible prophecy on which Christians will vary, and someday, we will all know who and what was right. But for now, thank you for joining me as we make our way through this possible chronology of the events that will take place during the last days.

CHAPTER 1

ISRAEL, GOD'S TIMEPIECE

While the subject of national Israel's place in the plan of God has long been debated, all debate should end with these verses:

Thus says the LORD,
who gives the sun for a light by day,
the ordinances of the moon and the stars for a light by night,
who disturbs the sea, and its waves roar
(the LORD of hosts is His name):

"If those ordinances depart
from before Me, says the LORD,
then the seed of Israel shall also cease
from being a nation before Me forever."

JEREMIAH 31:35-36

Earlier in the same chapter, the Lord says He will make a new covenant with the house of Israel—a covenant distinct from the one made after the exodus, one having to do with inward transformation rather than outward obligation:

> This is the covenant that I will make with the house of
> Israel after those days, says the LORD: I will put My law
> in their minds, and write it on their hearts; and I will be
> their God, and they shall be My people.

JEREMIAH 31:33

The central figure of Scripture is obviously the Messiah of Israel in the person of Jesus of Nazareth. But if we were to identify a second central character in Scripture, it would be national Israel. Though they were a people not great in number (Deuteronomy 7:7), they were chosen by God to bring the Messiah into the world. As church-age Christians, we know how the story goes concerning the people of Israel and their Messiah, and we also know that God's covenant with them as a national people group has yet to be fulfilled. Jeremiah was clearly writing about the return of Judah from the Babylonian captivity, yet his Spirit-inspired words were not limited to that time. We know that because there was no new covenant established after the Babylonian captivity; the nation still remained under the Mosaic law.

Beyond Israel's Messiah and Israel itself, Scripture also reveals a city associated with God's chosen people in connection with the last-days scenario:

> It shall happen in that day that I will make Jerusalem a
> very heavy stone for all peoples; all who would heave it
> away will surely be cut in pieces, though all nations of
> the earth are gathered against it.

ZECHARIAH 12:3

> Then the LORD will go forth
> and fight against those nations,
> as He fights in the day of battle.
> And in that day His feet will stand on the Mount of Olives,

which faces Jerusalem on the east.
And the Mount of Olives shall be split in two,
from east to west,
making a very large valley;
half of the mountain shall move toward the north
and half of it toward the south.

ZECHARIAH 14:3-4

"In that day" is a phrase used 16 times in Zechariah 12–14 and it is in reference to the great and terrible day of the Lord, the time of Jacob's trouble, or simply, the great tribulation, a time when God pours out His undiluted and direct wrath on the world. Zechariah mentions the people of the city in 12:2, which implies a people identified with the city, who obviously would be the Jews. Thus, we have a promise made of a future covenant with national Israel. We find the people associated with the city of Jerusalem mentioned in the last-days scenario by Zechariah, and we find God fighting against the nations who come against the city associated with God's people Israel. God has not cast off Israel, even though in the past, He scattered the Jewish people among the nations in judgment. He has not cast them off forever.

There are those today who hold to replacement theology, which teaches that the church has replaced Israel in God's redemptive plan. The problems with this view are many, not the least of which is the idea that God is done with the nation of Israel, when He's not. Another problem is that not all that is prophesied about the regathered people of God is positive. In other words, if some are going to claim that all the future blessings promised to Israel now apply to the church, then what about all the negative things prophesied about God's regathered people? They have to be fulfilled too, or the Bible contains errors. As the old saying goes, you have to take the good with the bad. If the church has replaced Israel, then the church is going through the tribulation. And if that is true, then the portions of the Bible that say the church will be raptured before the tribulation are wrong.

God has not cast off Israel, even though in the past, He scattered the Jewish people among the nations in judgment. He has not cast them off forever.

If the church has replaced Israel and thus is going through the tribulation, what do we do with passages like these?

> *1 Thessalonians 5:9*—"God did not appoint us to wrath, but to obtain salvation through our Lord Jesus Christ."

> *Revelation 3:10*—"Because you have kept My command to persevere, I also will keep you from the hour of trial which shall come upon the whole world, to test those who dwell on the earth."

The tribulation is the seventieth week in Daniel's prophecy of the 70 weeks. Like the other 69 seven-year periods, the seventieth week was also determined for Daniel's people and the holy city (Daniel 9:24). If the church has replaced Israel and Israel went through all of the first 69 weeks, then that means the church has to go through all of the seventieth week, or the tribulation. Then what do we do with 1 Thessalonians 5:9 and Revelation 3:10? To conclude that the church will go through the tribulation is to say that the rapture either doesn't happen or it will take place at the end of the tribulation. This view creates a host of other problems.

The regathering of Israel is central to eschatology and cannot be applied to the church, which has its own distinct prophecies and promises concerning the last days, some of which we will discuss later. First Thessalonians 5:9 and Revelation 3:10 shut the door on the possibility of the church going through the tribulation because the church is not appointed for wrath and will be kept from the hour of trial. Add to that the fact that from chapter 6 onward, the content of Revelation focuses on Israel and Christ-rejecting Gentiles. The obvious point is this: If Israel is mentioned in passages that are undeniably about the future, then Israel must exist in order for it to go through that prophesied time period.

The regathering of the Jews and the rebirth of the nation of Israel set off a series of events moving toward the day of the Lord and all that follows it—hence our chapter title, "Israel, God's Timepiece." If we are going to follow a chronological order of events that pertains to the last of the last days, we must begin with the regathering of the Jews into their land and the rebirth of the nation Israel. Jesus said,

> Now learn this parable from the fig tree: When its branch
> has already become tender and puts forth leaves, you know
> that summer is near. So you also, when you see all these
> things, know that it is near—at the doors! Assuredly, I say
> to you, this generation will by no means pass away till all
> these things take place. Heaven and earth will pass away,
> but My words will by no means pass away.
>
> MATTHEW 24:32-35

Hosea 9:10 and Joel 1:7 both metaphorically refer to Israel as a "fig tree," which tells us we are within the boundaries of Scripture to see this as referring to Israel. But there is even more compelling evidence that tells us not only can we see Israel as a fig tree, but we should.

The Olivet Discourse was taught during the Passion Week, the week leading up to Jesus' crucifixion on Passover. During that week,

Jesus made multiple trips into Jerusalem, beginning with the triumphal entry, when He received public worship as Israel's Messiah for the first time. It was on this day that He cleansed the temple and drove out the money changers and dove sellers.

> Now the next day, when they had come out from Bethany, He was hungry. And seeing from afar a fig tree having leaves, He went to see if perhaps He would find something on it. When He came to it, He found nothing but leaves, for it was not the season for figs. In response Jesus said to it, "Let no one eat fruit from you ever again." And His disciples heard it.
>
> MARK 11:12-14

> Now in the morning, as they passed by, they saw the fig tree dried up from the roots. And Peter, remembering, said to Him, "Rabbi, look! The fig tree which You cursed has withered away."
>
> MARK 11:20-21

It is almost universally agreed that the fig tree represented fruitless Israel, for at Jesus' first coming, it was not the season for the people of Israel to recognize their Messiah. That will occur at the second coming. Mark's Gospel gives us details not provided in Matthew and Luke, and by combining the eyewitness accounts, we can reach this conclusion (remembering that the fig tree represents unbelieving Israel). On Monday of the Passion Week, Jesus curses the fruitless fig tree, and on Tuesday, Jesus and His disciples encounter the same fig tree withered away, which pictures the scattering of the Jews among the nations and the nation ceasing to exist in its homeland. On the next day, Jesus says, "Learn this parable from the fig tree" (Matthew 24:32). He is talking to the same group of men, in the same city, about the same fig tree. Thus, if the fig tree represented unbelieving Israel on Monday and Tuesday, then on Wednesday the fig tree would still represent unbelieving Israel. We know from Ezekiel's vision in chapter 37 that Israel will be regathered into the land in national unbelief, so the metaphor of the fig tree is consistent in representing unbelieving Israel.

Jesus said, "Learn this parable from the fig tree: When its branch has already become tender and puts forth leaves [which comes before the fig tree bears fruit], you know that summer is near" (Matthew 24:32). He then clarifies the meaning of His words by saying the generation that sees the fig tree become tender and put forth leaves is the generation that will see all the things spoken of in the Olivet Discourse come to pass (verses 33-34). Within the span of a single generation, Israel will bud in unbelief (become a nation again), and before that generation passes away, the people will look upon the one whom they pierced and mourn as one mourns for an only son (Zechariah 12:10). This is the fruit that will grow after the leaves bud, which will happen at the second coming.

We also find evidence of the necessity of a regathered nation of Israel in the last days from this prophecy in Daniel:

> Seventy weeks are determined
> for your people and for your holy city,
> to finish the transgression,
> to make an end of sins,
> to make reconciliation for iniquity,
> to bring in everlasting righteousness,
> to seal up vision and prophecy,
> and to anoint the Most Holy.
>
> **DANIEL 9:24**

Daniel, in prayer, says, "Lord, we have transgressed—we have sinned and committed iniquity." In response, the Lord says He will "make an end of sins...make reconciliation for iniquity, to bring in everlasting righteousness." In verses 25-27, God tells Daniel when and how He is going to do those things through the two advents of Jesus. There is much discussion among scholars about these verses—some seek to apply them to the church, others see them as allegorical, and still others see them as strictly historical.

Gabriel's words in Daniel 9:24 settle all the debates when he says, "Seventy weeks are determined for your [Daniel's] people and your holy city." The Hebrew word translated "determined" is interesting—its primary meaning is "to cut off." This means there is a cut-off point after the 70 weeks expire. It can also be translated as "to be settled" or "to mark out."

Therefore, it cannot mean 69 weeks and then the church will replace Israel. Nor can it mean the first 69 weeks will be literal and the seventieth week allegorical. Gabriel was saying to Daniel, "In answer to your supplication regarding your people, there is marked out a period of seventy weeks for them."

For us, the use of *week* leads us to think of seven days. To Daniel and his people the Jews, the word translated "week"—*shabua*—meant a period of sevens, which could be days or years.

So that we can better understand the significance of this 70 weeks' prophecy, let's go back to Leviticus:

> The LORD spoke to Moses on Mount Sinai, saying, "Speak
> to the children of Israel, and say to them: 'When you come
> into the land which I give you, then the land shall keep
> a sabbath to the LORD. Six years you shall sow your field,
> and six years you shall prune your vineyard, and gather
> its fruit; but in the seventh year there shall be a sabbath
> of solemn rest for the land, a sabbath to the LORD. You
> shall neither sow your field nor prune your vineyard. What
> grows of its own accord of your harvest you shall not reap,

nor gather the grapes of your untended vine, for it is a
year of rest for the land.'"

LEVITICUS 25:1-5

After six years of planting and harvesting, the people of Israel were
to let the land rest for a year. But they didn't. This helps us to understand the 70 years of captivity in Babylon, which resulted from the
people's disobedience and God's subsequent judgment:

> They burned the house of God, broke down the wall of
> Jerusalem, burned all its palaces with fire, and destroyed
> all its precious possessions. And those who escaped from
> the sword he carried away to Babylon, where they became
> servants to him and his sons until the rule of the kingdom
> of Persia, to fulfill the word of the LORD by the mouth of
> Jeremiah, until the land had enjoyed her Sabbaths. As long
> as she lay desolate she kept Sabbath, to fulfill seventy years.

2 CHRONICLES 36:19-21

Israel had transgressed and ignored the sabbatical year for 490 years,
or a total of 70 Sabbath years. That is what determined the duration
of the Babylonian captivity as 70 years. Therefore, the weeks spoken
of to Daniel refer to weeks of *years*, because it was weeks of years that
determined the length of Israel's captivity. Gabriel said 490 years were
determined, then transgression would be finished. An end would be
brought to sin, with reconciliation to righteousness. This speaks of
the finished work of Christ on the cross at His first coming. Remember that Jesus came to the Jews first (Romans 1:16).

Daniel was told the 70 weeks will happen in three parts: 7 weeks,
62 weeks, then one week. Each week represents a period of seven
years. Then he was given these details about the middle section of
62 weeks:

After the sixty-two weeks
Messiah shall be cut off, but not for Himself;
and the people of the prince who is to come
shall destroy the city and the sanctuary.
The end of it shall be with a flood,
and till the end of the war desolations are determined.
Then he shall confirm a covenant with many for one week;
but in the middle of the week
he shall bring an end to sacrifice and offering.
And on the wing of abominations shall be one
who makes desolate,
even until the consummation, which is determined,
is poured out on the desolate.

DANIEL 9:26-27

The first section, 7 weeks, ended with the rebuilding of the wall around Jerusalem as recorded in Nehemiah. The 69 weeks ended with the Messiah's triumphal entry into Jerusalem. Then we are told of a covenant made by the "people of the prince who is to come." In chapter 7, we will talk about who this refers to, but for now, we need to note that there is a "one week" (or seven-year) covenant that not only has yet to be fulfilled, it has yet to be made. We must also note that the context is the same as that of verse 24, where the determined weeks pertain to Daniel's people and holy city, the Jews and Jerusalem, and therefore, the covenant must be made with the same.

Gabriel doesn't say that when God's people take dominion over the earth the Messiah will come and make reconciliation, as taught by some. He doesn't say that when man finally starts to get it right, sin will end. Rather, Gabriel says the end is already determined, and Israel is the timepiece by which that time can be identified.

In Amos 9:14-15, God says,

> I will bring back the captives of My people Israel; They
> shall build the waste cities and inhabit them; They shall
> plant vineyards and drink wine from them; they shall also
> make gardens and eat fruit from them. I will plant them
> in their land, and no longer shall they be pulled up from
> the land I have given them.

Israel has rebuilt and inhabited cities that were originally a waste-
land and planted vineyards and built wineries. Today there are more
than 35 commercial wineries in Israel, and more than 250 boutique
wineries.

God's prophetic word about Israel is being fulfilled
in and through Israel right before our eyes.

Is Israel a fruit-producing nation as prophesied by Amos? Israel
exports $1.3 billion dollars of fruit every year, mostly citrus, and is
one of the leading greenhouse fruit producers in the world. God's
prophetic word about Israel is being fulfilled in and through Israel
right before our eyes.

In His Olivet Discourse, Jesus gave us a glimpse of what will happen during the seventieth week:

> "Therefore when you see the 'abomination of desolation,'
> spoken of by Daniel the prophet, standing in the holy
> place" (whoever reads, let him understand), "then let those
> who are in Judea flee to the mountains. Let him who is
> on the housetop not go down to take anything out of his
> house. And let him who is in the field not go back to get
> his clothes. But woe to those who are pregnant and to

those who are nursing babies in those days! And pray that your flight may not be in winter or on the Sabbath. For then there will be great tribulation, such as has not been since the beginning of the world until this time, no, nor ever shall be. And unless those days were shortened, no flesh would be saved; but for the elect's sake those days will be shortened."

MATTHEW 24:15-22

God said sin must end and man cannot and will never end it, so God will. All 70 weeks pertain to the Jews and Jerusalem, and only 69 have been fulfilled so far. The seventieth week is yet to come. Again, the weeks are determined—they are set and marked out; there is no other interpretation or negotiation about what this means. The last days of life on earth as we know it have to do with the Jews and Jerusalem. This is predetermined. The march to the fulfillment of all the prophecies concerning the last days, which does not include the millennium, began when Israel budded and put forth leaves, which means that within one season, Israel would become fruitful.

> The Lord will save the tents of Judah first, so that the glory of the house of David and the glory of the inhabitants of Jerusalem shall not become greater than that of Judah. In that day the Lord will defend the inhabitants of Jerusalem; the one who is feeble among them in that day shall be like David, and the house of David shall be like God, like the Angel of the Lord before them. It shall be in that day that I will seek to destroy all the nations that come against Jerusalem.
>
> And I will pour on the house of David and on the inhabitants of Jerusalem the Spirit of grace and supplication; then they

will look on Me whom they pierced. Yes, they will mourn
for Him as one mourns for his only son, and grieve for
Him as one grieves for a firstborn.

ZECHARIAH 12:7-10

The fact that the seventieth week of Daniel is associated with the
Jews and Jerusalem is as sure as the fact there is a God in heaven—
the same God who set the 70 weeks in a predetermined order: 7
weeks, then 62 weeks, then a gap of time, then 1 week. The seventieth week is the one Zechariah speaks of, and the one Gabriel tells
of. It is the one week that, if it were not limited to 7 years, no flesh
would survive. It is the time of Jacob's trouble, the great and terrible day of the Lord, and there is no way to make that week apply
to the church. Remember what we read a moment ago from Amos:

> "I will bring back the captives of My people Israel;
> they shall build the waste cities and inhabit them;
> they shall plant vineyards and drink wine from them;
> they shall also make gardens and eat fruit from them.
> I will plant them in their land,
> and no longer shall they be pulled up
> from the land I have given them,"
> says the LORD your God.

AMOS 9:14-15

The point Amos makes for us is crucial to understanding the
prophetic time line of the last days. Though Amos was a contempo-
rary of Hosea and Isaiah, we know that what Amos wrote in chapter
9 of his prophecy does not pertain to the return of the Jewish cap-
tives from Babylon to Jerusalem. We know this because of what he
describes did *not* happen. The Jews did return from their Babylonian

captivity; they did build the waste cities, plant vineyards and gardens, and eat and drink from them. But they were "pulled up" from the land for nearly 2,000 years. This reveals that Amos's prophecy was not fully fulfilled in the past. Therefore, the complete fulfillment is yet future. We are living in the days when this is being fulfilled. The national people group with the ethnic identity, language, heritage, and history of the biblical Jews are now back in the land, and this has begun the fulfillment of what Amos wrote. This means no matter how various world governments and the UN may try to uproot Israel from the land, God Himself will not allow that to happen. The reason this is crucial to the prophetic time line is that the promise is specific to an identifiable people group who are the second most significant figures in Scripture, the Jews.

If the Jews weren't to return from being scattering amongst the nations, and they weren't brought back into the same geographic region of the world in which Jerusalem is located, then God would not have kept His promises to them, and that would be catastrophic for us all! For those who claim that modern Israel is not biblical Israel, I would ask: Then why is everything written about biblical Israel by the prophets happening to the modern state of Israel? Why is the world gathered against her? Why are there efforts to divide the city of Jerusalem? Why is the city a burdensome stone to all the nations? The fact is, Israel's existence today confirms the fulfillment of prophecies that tell us God's prophetic clock is moving toward its foretold end. Israel is the timepiece by which last-days events can be measured.

Israel's existence today confirms the fulfillment
of prophecies that tell us God's prophetic
clock is moving toward its foretold end.

Gabriel told Daniel there is coming a seven-year period for his people and Jerusalem that is yet unfulfilled. It requires the Jews be a national people group, that they be in Israel, and that they have possession of all of Jerusalem. All these things have taken place within the span of a single generation, and that generation is coming to an end. "How long is a generation?" is a popular question, and there are several answers people have come up with, but the truth is we don't know. What we do know is there is only one generation, and the same way that the fig tree will bud and bear fruit within the same season, so too will Israel.

One last point before we move on: There are some who say God has cast off Israel forever, but the following passages say otherwise:

> The LORD will go forth
> and fight against those nations,
> as He fights in the day of battle.
> And in that day His feet will stand on the Mount of Olives,
> which faces Jerusalem on the east.
> And the Mount of Olives shall be split in two,
> from east to west,
> making a very large valley;
> half of the mountain shall move toward the north
> and half of it toward the south.

ZECHARIAH 14:3-4

> It shall come to pass that everyone who is left of all the nations which came against Jerusalem shall go up from year to year to worship the King, the LORD of hosts, and to keep the Feast of Tabernacles.

ZECHARIAH 14:16

> I saw a new heaven and a new earth, for the first heaven and the first earth had passed away. Also there was no

more sea. Then I, John, saw the holy city, New Jerusalem, coming down out of heaven from God, prepared as a bride adorned for her husband.

REVELATION 21:1-2

If God has cast off the nation of Israel forever, as some people say, then why is Jesus returning to the Mount of Olives, which faces Jerusalem from the east? Why will He rule and reign during the millennium from Jerusalem? And why, after the old heaven and earth have passed away, will the holy city be called the New Jerusalem? If it's true God has cast off Israel, then it doesn't make sense that the Lord would come back to Israel, rule from Israel during the millennium, and call the holy city that descends from heaven the New Jerusalem.

Modern Israel is biblical Israel. There is no other explanation for the nation's existence other than to fulfill what is yet unfulfilled in the prophecies concerning God's chosen people, the Jews.

So now that there is a nation of Israel and the chosen people of God are returning to their covenanted homeland in record numbers, what's next? The next chapter will fill in those details. But for now, we can conclude that we are living in the generation that will not pass away until all the prophecies Jesus presented in the Olivet Discourse are fulfilled.

CHAPTER 2

THE TIME OF THE SIGNS

When it comes to Bible passages relating to eschatology, commentators have held to different interpretations and meanings of what they believe Scripture says about the end times. This includes their views on the private briefing Jesus had with four of His disciples on the subject of the signs of His coming. They have debated how Jesus' words in Matthew 24 and 25 should be understood. Jesus' teaching took place during the passion week and was shared with the pair of fishermen brothers who were among the twelve—Peter, Andrew, James, and John. The conversation is recorded by Matthew and Luke, and it is Matthew's record that we will use to examine the content and context of what Jesus said. Here's how the conversation opens:

> Jesus went out and departed from the temple, and His disciples came up to show Him the buildings of the temple. And Jesus said to them, "Do you not see all these things? Assuredly, I say to you, not one stone shall be left here upon another, that shall not be thrown down." Now as He sat on the Mount of Olives, the disciples came to

Him privately, saying, "Tell us, when will these things
be? And what will be the sign of Your coming, and of
the end of the age?"

MATTHEW 24:1-3

Luke tells us the inquiry posed to Jesus by the pair of fisherman
brothers was threefold: When will the temple be destroyed, what
sign will indicate Your return is near, and what signs will signal the
end of the age? What's interesting about Jesus' longest of answers to
any question asked of Him is that He never addressed the issue of
the destruction of the temple (not one stone being left here upon
another). The reason this is important to note is that it separates that
event from the answer Jesus gave. Historically, we know that the temple was destroyed by the Romans in AD 70, but we also know that
the other events mentioned by Jesus did not happen at that same
time. This indicates the destruction of the temple would be a separate event from those mentioned in the Olivet Discourse. This is key
to our interpretation of the passage when we encounter those who
say everything recorded in the Olivet Discourse was fulfilled in AD
70. Textually, this is not possible, as Jesus did not include the AD 70
destruction of the temple in His answer, and to say all else written
in the discourse applies to that same time requires eisegesis (inserting
one's presuppositions into the interpretation of the text), which is a
dangerous practice when it comes to interpreting Scripture.

Note carefully what Jesus said would take place upon His return:

> Immediately after the tribulation of those days the sun will
> be darkened, and the moon will not give its light; the stars
> will fall from heaven, and the powers of the heavens will
> be shaken. Then the sign of the Son of Man will appear
> in heaven, and then all the tribes of the earth will mourn,
> and they will see the Son of Man coming on the clouds

of heaven with power and great glory. And He will send
His angels with a great sound of a trumpet, and they will
gather together His elect from the four winds, from one
end of heaven to the other.

MATTHEW 24:29-31

Since it is clear none of these things happened in AD 70, some
people have chosen to allegorize them into some kind of spiritual
application or figurative meaning because of their belief that the
Olivet Discourse is not prophecy. But the context will not allow this
in light of the fact that this was not a teaching per se, but was more of
an intelligence briefing in which Jesus was revealing the future of the
world to the quartet of disciples. Jesus went on to teach two parables
in Matthew 25 to illustrate what the mindsets of the Jews and mankind will be like at the time of the fulfillment of the Olivet Discourse.

In light of the fact that I hold to the pre-tribulation rapture view,
I do not believe that most of the content of the Olivet Discourse has
any application for the church, outside of motivating us to share the
gospel with as many people as we can, including the Jews, because
of what is coming upon the whole world. I do not believe, however,
that everything in the Olivet Discourse is limited to the seventieth
week of Daniel or the tribulation or specifically to the Jews.

The group of disciples who posed the questions in Matthew 24:3
to Jesus were a unique group. They were Jews, and also founding
members of the church. Because the questions were posed about the
future, and the future would include nearly 2,000 years of church
history—and because two of the men who asked the questions, Peter
and John, would play significant roles in the early church—we are
not imposing on Scripture when we conclude that the answer Jesus
gave would include information about the latter days of church history prior to the seventieth week of Daniel. In fact, when we study
Scripture, two of the crucial elements in interpreting the content are

(1) who is speaking? and (2) who is being spoken to? In the Olivet Discourse, the Holy One of Israel, who is also the head of the church, is speaking to four Jewish disciples who were also among the 12 apostles of the church. With that in mind, we can move forward.

> Of that day and hour no one knows, not even the angels of heaven, but My Father only. But as the days of Noah were, so also will the coming of the Son of Man be. For as in the days before the flood, they were eating and drinking, marrying and giving in marriage, until the day that Noah entered the ark, and did not know until the flood came and took them all away, so also will the coming of the Son of Man be. Then two men will be in the field: one will be taken and the other left. Two women will be grinding at the mill: one will be taken and the other left. Watch therefore, for you do not know what hour your Lord is coming.
>
> MATTHEW 24:36-42

Jesus told the disciples in John 14:3 that He would "come again" for the purpose of taking them up and receiving them to Himself so that where He is, they may be also. This must refer to the rapture, because Revelation 19:11-16 makes it clear that the church returns to earth with Jesus at the second coming. The day and hour when this will happen is unknown.

The second coming is a bit different in that we know the length of the tribulation, or the seventieth week of Daniel, is 84 30-day months, or 2,520 days divided into two 1,260-day portions. We also know that at the 1,260-day mark, the abomination of desolation will be committed. That's when the antichrist will claim to be God and sit in the most holy place of the biblically unsanctioned third temple. It is from that point in time onward that we know the return of

Christ will occur in 1,260 days. The point is that the timing of the second coming is not completely unknown, though Scripture does not clearly state how soon after the rapture the tribulation will begin.

In light of this, "the days before the flood" in Matthew 24:38 should be understood as the time before God poured out His wrath on the whole earth. That means Jesus is saying that at the end of the church age, before the tribulation begins, things will be like they were in Noah's day. The days before the flood are described as a time of indifference to the impending signs of coming judgment. This indifference is said to be illustrated by buying and selling, marrying and giving in marriage. Many see this as a description of life on earth prior to the second coming, but this is beyond unlikely. Revelation 18 tells us specifically what will be happening on the earth right before the second coming of Jesus:

> A mighty angel took up a stone like a great millstone and threw it into the sea, saying, "Thus with violence the great city Babylon shall be thrown down, and shall not be found anymore. The sound of harpists, musicians, flutists, and trumpeters shall not be heard in you anymore. No craftsman of any craft shall be found in you anymore, and the sound of a millstone shall not be heard in you anymore. The light of a lamp shall not shine in you anymore, and the voice of bridegroom and bride shall not be heard in you anymore. For your merchants were the great men of the earth, for by your sorcery all the nations were deceived."
>
> **REVELATION 18:21-23**

At the end of the tribulation, right before the return of Christ, there will be a global economic collapse, with no buying and selling and no marrying and giving in marriage, as indicated by the voice of the bridegroom and bride not being heard any longer repeating their vows. That means that "the days before the flood" are pointing to what life will be like in the days before God's global wrath while the church is still present on the earth. In the time prior to the time of tribulation like the world has never seen, mankind will be indifferent to the clear signs of imminent and impending judgment and will have a "life goes on" and "business as usual" kind of attitude.

During that time, "two men will be in the field: one will be taken and the other left. Two women will be grinding at the mill: one will be taken and the other left. Watch therefore, for you do not know what hour your Lord is coming" (Matthew 24:40-42). Again, that statement cannot refer to the second coming because the day and hour of the second coming can be determined once the abomination of desolation occurs—which is exactly 1,260 days after the tribulation begins, and the second coming of Jesus is 1,260 days after that.

The other point to note is that at the time of the second coming, no one will be working in the field, and no one will be grinding at the mill. In fact, according to Revelation 12:6, the Jews will have fled to the place in the wilderness that the Lord has prepared for them. They will be there until the second coming, or for 1,260 days.

Therefore, it is plausible, or even likely, that the "one person taken, one person left" description in Matthew 24:40-41 refers to the rapture of the church and is not a parallel passage to Matthew 25:32-33, which talks about the dividing of the sheep and the goats. Nor is it a reference to some people being taken to hell and others left on earth. We know this because the context is determined by the "days before the flood" statement made by Jesus. That is when one will be taken and the other left. One will be taken to be with the Lord where He is, and the other will be left to endure the tribulation.

The question, then, is this: What can we know about the days of Noah outside of the business-as-usual attitude that will be predominant at the time before God's final judgment and the rapture of the church? Here is what Genesis 6 tells us:

The LORD saw that the wickedness of man was great in the earth, and that every intent of the thoughts of his heart was only evil continually.

GENESIS 6:5

The earth also was corrupt before God, and the earth was filled with violence. So God looked upon the earth, and indeed it was corrupt; for all flesh had corrupted their way on the earth.

And God said to Noah, "The end of all flesh has come before Me, for the earth is filled with violence through them; and behold, I will destroy them with the earth."

GENESIS 6:11-13

I need not try to convince anyone that we live in a violent world, or that man's heart is filled with the constant pursuit of evil. The word "corrupt" in Genesis 6:12, however, will help us see that we are indeed living in times that are like those of Noah. The word means "moral perversion." It is the word we would use to describe meat or fruit that was rotten or spoiled. In the days before the flood, mankind had few or no moral values, for they had essentially rotted away.

At the time of this writing, there are efforts around the world, in many first-world countries, to indoctrinate elementary school-aged children with the belief that transgenderism and homosexuality are as natural and acceptable in society as heterosexuality. There is even a movement to normalize pedophilia as a natural sexual attraction and preference. Children are being force-fed the idea that rather than following the scientific facts that gender is biologically and genetically determined, gender is actually a choice. The latest fad among liberal, progressive parents is "gender neutral" child-rearing, and letting their child choose their gender when ready.

We live in a time when people are told their feelings can define their gender, and prepubescent children are having their little bodies altered surgically because they told their deluded parents they "feel" like the opposite gender than they are. There have always been tomboys and effeminate boys, but neither of those tendencies have ever indicated that their chromosomal arrangement was wrong. Yet today, the "trust the science" crowd doesn't trust the science, and they place feelings above facts even when it comes to undeniable biological and physiological realities. To give prepubescent children puberty blockers or to surgically alter their bodies shows how far astray mankind has gone from God's original design of creating male and female in Genesis 1:27. What we see happening today is part of the thoughts and intents of man's heart being evil continually, as it was in the days of Noah.

On another front, multiple state legislatures are repealing parental notification rights and allowing for girls to be taken off campus to have an abortion without their parents' knowledge. Many other states are expanding abortion rights up to the moment of birth, and some are even promoting post-birth abortions that deny any medical aid to an abortion-surviving baby. States are repealing laws that criminalize physical assaults that cause the death of an unborn child. My home state of California is even offering to help underage girls cross state lines, without the knowledge of their parents, to have an abortion if their home state does not allow it after *Roe v. Wade* was repealed. This, by the way, is normally a felony, yet because the issue is abortion, officials approve of the change and look the other way.

This tells us that man has become morally corrupt to the degree that most have lost any sort of moral compass, and objective realities are treated as subjective interpretations. We live in a day when it is as it was at the time of Noah and evil intentions fill the minds of humanity.

We live in a day when it is as it was at the time of
Noah and evil intentions fill the minds of humanity.

While it is true, as I mentioned earlier, that there is little need to convince anyone that we live in a violent world, we only need mention groups like ISIS or Boko Haram to make the point about how horrible violence has become. The violence of the last days, however, will move beyond what we see from ideological or religiously motivated hate groups. Jesus gives us specifics about what will be happening with increasing frequency and intensity in the last days prior to His coming for the church.

> Now as He sat on the Mount of Olives, the disciples came to Him privately, saying, "Tell us, when will these things be? And what will be the sign of Your coming, and of the end of the age?" And Jesus answered and said to them: "Take heed that no one deceives you. For many will come in My name, saying, 'I am the Christ,' and will deceive many. And you will hear of wars and rumors of wars. See that you are not troubled; for all these things must come to pass, but the end is not yet. For nation will rise against nation, and kingdom against kingdom. And there will be famines, pestilences, and earthquakes in various places. All these are the beginning of sorrows."
>
> **MATTHEW 24:3-8**

Garden-variety Bible critics and preterists (those who believe that some or all of the Bibles prophecies about the end times have been fulfilled) often point out that false Christs, wars and rumors of wars, international and ethnic tensions, famines, pestilence (meaning plagues), and earthquakes have always been a part of life on earth. However, because the question the disciples asked was in relation to the last days and not just the course of human history, and because the disciples asked about signs relating to Christ's return, we know that Jesus' answer about these normal course-of-life events relates exclusively to the last days. I believe this is confirmed in Jesus' use of the phrase "beginning of sorrows" (Matthew 24:8).

Note also what Paul wrote:

> Concerning the times and the seasons, brethren, you have no need that I should write to you. For you yourselves know perfectly that the day of the Lord so comes as a thief in the night. For when they say, "Peace and safety!" then sudden destruction comes upon them, as labor pains upon a pregnant woman. And they shall not escape. But you, brethren, are not in darkness, so that this Day should overtake you as a thief. You are all sons of light and sons of the day. We are not of the night nor of darkness.
>
> 1 THESSALONIANS 5:1-5

Paul indicates clearly that for the Christian, there is an awareness of the lateness of the hour even though the day and hour cannot be known. The word "pains" here is the same Greek word translated as "sorrows" in Matthew 24:8. The word "beginning" in Matthew 24:8 could also be translated "commencement." With all that said, we can know that Jesus was telling His inquirers about the signs that indicate His return is near. There is coming a day when birth pangs will commence, and as we know, once labor pains begin in earnest, there is no reversing the process.

That means that after the fig tree puts forth leaves (after Israel becomes a nation once again), false Christs will abound and increase. It is important to remember Christ means "anointed" here. I don't think we need to read this as referring to a myriad of people claiming to be Christ Himself at the second coming, but rather, that we will see an increase in the numbers of those who use Jesus' name to claim an anointing on their ministry. We'll talk more about this in the next chapter. This claim cannot apply to the tribulation, for there will be one false Christ during the tribulation, not many.

If we are in the last of the last days, we would expect to see threats of war on the rise globally and an increase in military conflicts around the world. "Nation will rise against nation" has a twofold meaning. The Greek word for nation is *ethnos*, from which we derive our word *ethnic*. It also can refer to nations who worship gods other than the God of the Bible. Therefore, after Israel becomes a nation again, ethnic and religious tensions will be on the rise. "Kingdom against kingdom" speaks of international strife, and "famines" means just what we think: a shortage of food supplies. "Pestilence" can also be translated as "plagues," and we would expect to see a rise in diseases after Israel became a nation. The last of the birth pangs that will increase in frequency and intensity after Israel becomes a nation is *seismos*, translated as "earthquakes." The word can also mean a tempest or gale, and thus we would expect to see a rise in catastrophic geological events as well as unprecedented weather anomalies after the Jews are back in their land.

We could fill the rest of this book with statistics and data concerning the increase of all these things since 1948, but I will leave that for you to research on your own, if you'd like. I believe there is sufficient evidence for anyone over 30 that these things have increased dramatically in recent years. Start reading news stories and watch for the term *unprecedented*, and see how often it comes up. Watch for phrases that indicate the rarity or unusual intensity of a normal phenomenon—like a once-in-every-thousand-years flood, or once-in-every-five-hundred-years earthquake. The news is filled with such phrases, indicating that events the earth has always experienced are happening at unusually intense levels and frequencies.

We could cite the stats regarding wars and rumors of wars, or the increase of pestilence and how often we are hearing about food shortages and supply-chain problems. But again, based on what we see taking place around us, no one would deny that these problems are happening with increasing frequency and intensity.

The "commencement of birth pangs" is well underway, and the "heavy labor" portion of this process will happen during the tribulation. That's when a global famine will sweep the earth, according to Revelation 6:5, and when an earthquake of a magnitude never recorded in history will take place, as stated in Revelation 16:18. Then the world will finally give birth to the millennial reign of Christ on earth.

The phrase "commencement of labor pains" is important for two reasons: (1) real labor is irreversible, and (2) real labor is identifiable. A woman does not find out she's in labor when the heavy labor portion begins. Rather, when the pains commence, they begin a series of transitions that eventually arrive at the time to give birth. The pains at the end are the most intense, and this is exactly what's going to happen during the tribulation. Labor pains will begin beforehand, and they will grow more frequent and intense as they progress.

We are living in the time of the signs that Jesus identified for the four disciples who asked what to look for when His coming was near. We will look at these signs further in the next two chapters as we examine them from two perspectives: signs in the world, and signs in the church.

CHAPTER 3

SIGNS IN
THE WORLD

I n the Bible, we are given a detailed picture of coming events that will take place at the end of the church age, the time of the tribulation, and into the millennium and eternity.

The details we are given about the morality and mindset of the world during the tribulation give us a general idea of how close we are to that time that is coming upon the whole world. This is why it is such a tragedy that so many pastors or teachers today shy away from teaching Bible prophecy. Or, they do the opposite and sensationalize Bible prophecy. Prophecy should not be ignored, nor should it be sensationalized. The former leaves people unaware of how close we are and the sense of urgency they should have for the lost and dying around them, and the other leaves people misinformed and disappointed when what was presented as "the next big thing in the prophetic calendar" doesn't happen. We have sufficient information to tell us the lateness of the hour, and teaching a literal approach to interpreting Bible prophecy will be sensational enough. We don't need any additives to pique people's interest.

Now let's turn our attention to an important point made in Revelation 6:

> I looked when He opened the sixth seal, and behold, there was a great earthquake; and the sun became black as sackcloth of hair, and the moon became like blood. And the stars of heaven fell to the earth, as a fig tree drops its late figs when it is shaken by a mighty wind. Then the sky receded as a scroll when it is rolled up, and every mountain and island was moved out of its place. And the kings of the earth, the great men, the rich men, the commanders, the mighty men, every slave and every free man, hid themselves in the caves and in the rocks of the mountains, and said to the mountains and rocks, "Fall on us and hide us from the face of Him who sits on the throne and from the wrath of the Lamb! For the great day of His wrath has come, and who is able to stand?"
>
> **REVELATION 6:12-17**

Up to this time during the tribulation, the famed four horsemen of the apocalypse have ridden onto the world scene. The antichrist has made a covenant with Israel, and the Middle East crisis has been resolved. (Or so the world thinks.) The pseudo-peace the man of sin brings into the world will be short-lived as people begin killing one another when the rider on the fiery red horse is released. Unprecedented global famine will then sweep the world as the rider on the black mount—with scales in his hand—pushes the price of a loaf of bread to a day's pay. (Think about how often we are hearing about grain prices due to the Russia-Ukraine war.) This opens the door to the last of the four horsemen, the rider on the pale green horse, whose name is Death. He is followed by Hades, and a fourth of the world's population will die under his ride of terror as he kills by the sword, hunger, and the beasts of the earth.

The opening of the fifth seal reveals a multitude who were killed by the antichrist. These martyrs are in heaven, waiting on the Lord to avenge their blood on "those who dwell on the earth" (Revelation 6:10). The opening of the sixth seal leads to cosmic and geological events that leave people from every walk and status of life calling to the mountains and rocks to hide them from the wrath of Him who sits on the throne and the wrath of the Lamb. Thankfully, we will see none of these things, for we do not have an appointment with God's wrath (1 Thessalonians 5:9).

The point is this, those who would rather call out to the creation (mountains and rocks) than call on their creator—even though they know they are under the judgment of God—will expose the very reason they are in the tribulation in the first place. Paul explains how people arrive at this spiritual condition in the opening chapter of Romans:

> Since the creation of the world His invisible attributes are clearly seen, being understood by the things that are made, even His eternal power and Godhead, so that they are without excuse, because, although they knew God, they did not glorify Him as God, nor were thankful, but became futile in their thoughts, and their foolish hearts were darkened.
>
> **ROMANS 1:20-21**

God's invisible attributes are clearly seen and understood by the things that are made—to the degree that they invalidate every person's excuse for denying there is a God. Those who take the position of denying God as creator, even though He is the only possible explanation for how everything came into being, refuse to give Him glory. Nor are they thankful to Him. The result is they become futile in their thoughts and their foolish hearts are darkened. The Greek word translated "futile" means morally wicked and idolatrous.

This tells us the mentally and morally corrupt people who call out to the mountains and rocks to hide them arrived at that condition before the tribulation began, which is the very reason they find themselves in the midst of it. That gives us a hint at what the world will be like prior to the rapture of the church and the ensuing tribulation. People will deny the existence of God in spite of the overwhelming evidence that He exists. It is fitting that we ask the age-old question, Are we there yet? The answer comes in the question, Has the majority of the world rejected the existence of God, or replaced the God of the Bible with their own deity? In both cases, the answer is a resounding yes! The signs that the world is ready and willing for the man of sin to rule them are all around us.

One of the primary reasons atheists give for denying God is what they claim to be a lack of evidence for His existence. The reasons they arrive at their conclusion are (1) where they look, and (2) the terms they set. They often frame their rejection in a series of "How could a God of love do this?" questions. How could a God of love allow disease, or the death of children, or war, or hell? Their claim is that these things are inconsistent with their terms as to who or what God should be. What they fail to realize and accept is that this life is not all there is, and there is coming an eternal existence where all the things they call into question will no longer exist.

> Now I saw a new heaven and a new earth, for the first heaven and the first earth had passed away. Also there was no more sea. Then I, John, saw the holy city, New Jerusalem, coming down out of heaven from God, prepared as a bride adorned for her husband. And I heard a loud voice from heaven saying, "Behold, the tabernacle of God is with men, and He will dwell with them, and they shall be His people. God Himself will be with them and be their God. And God will wipe away every tear from their

eyes; there shall be no more death, nor sorrow, nor crying. There shall be no more pain, for the former things have passed away."

REVELATION 21:1-4

The arguments made by the God deniers would have some credence if heaven were not made accessible to all through Jesus Christ. Yet even though the evidence from the research done by those in the various scientific disciplines points to intelligent design and thus a designer, they still deny the evidence, and their hearts are hardened to the degree that they will not repent. This will especially be true during the tribulation, even when the God deniers realize they are under the direct wrath of God. Thus, if we are seeing the signs come to pass, and the number of God deniers is growing by leaps and bounds, then the only rightful conclusion must be that the Day of the Lord is at hand.

We live in a time when the most intolerant people in society are those who demand Christians tolerate whatever others think is true.

Today, Christianity is the one "religion" that is viewed as negative by many. It is the one belief system that infuriates people like no other. People are more tolerant of Islam (which means "submission") than they are of Christianity (which means "Christlike"). Jesus warned that we can expect to face hostility:

If the world hates you, you know that it hated Me before it hated you. If you were of the world, the world would

love its own. Yet because you are not of the world, but I
chose you out of the world, therefore the world hates you.

JOHN 15:18-19

The rising dislike of Christianity—and thus Christians—is directly
related to the increase of moral depravity in our world. We live in
a time when the most intolerant people in society are those who
demand Christians tolerate whatever others think is true. Yet they
will not tolerate anyone who disagrees with them, especially Christians. This is why, during the tribulation, people will cry out to the
rocks and mountains rather than repent of their sin—even though
they realize the world is experiencing God's wrath.

The apostle Paul gives us more insight into the direction the world
is trending:

> The coming of the lawless one is according to the working
> of Satan, with all power, signs, and lying wonders, and
> with all unrighteous deception among those who perish,
> because they did not receive the love of the truth, that
> they might be saved. And for this reason God will send
> them strong delusion, that they should believe the lie,
> that they all may be condemned who did not believe
> the truth but had pleasure in unrighteousness.

2 THESSALONIANS 2:9-12

The word "delusion" means "fraudulence." It can also refer to
straying mentally, a wrong opinion relative to morals or religion, an
error that shows itself in action, or a wrong mode of acting. The "lie"
believed by the people mentioned in 2 Thessalonians 2:11-12 is the
antichrist's claim that he is God, the world's Savior and Lord. Are
we seeing the world move in the direction of the ultimate lie being

believed by the masses? Do people have the wrong opinions today with regard to morals or religion? Are these errors manifesting themselves in the actions of the deluded? Have many in our world mentally strayed from the truth and facts? Are people today looking to the government or powerful leaders to lead and save them from life debts, burdens, and perils?

I think we all know the answers to those questions. We live in a time when the level of mental straying from long-held and obvious truths tells us we are near the end of the church age and approaching the tribulation. We have become familiar with new terms being invented to accommodate the beliefs of a deluded world. *Gender dysphoria* is one of those terms. This refers to the condition of feeling one's emotional and psychological identity as male or female is the opposite of one's biological sex. The key word here is *feelings*; the individual's gender is determined by their feelings and not the facts of genetics and biology. This indicates a mental straying from what is actually true. In other words, you can use orange spray paint on an apple and try calling it an orange, but it won't change it from being an apple. You can give hormone treatments to a man and put him in a dress and high heels, but if you look at his chromosomes, they are still XY, and therefore he is still male, no matter how he may feel. But, if you don't accept such a person or call them by their preferred pronouns, you could lose your job and, in some places, go to jail. Think about how far that strays from genetic and biological truth— the possibility of being fired or imprisoned for not calling a boy a girl or a woman a man.

As we mentioned in chapter 2, Jesus made a parallel between "the days before the flood" and the times preceding the rapture. One of the dominant characteristics of Noah's days was corruption.

> The earth also was corrupt before God, and the earth was
> filled with violence. So God looked upon the earth, and

indeed it was corrupt; for all flesh had corrupted their way on the earth.

GENESIS 6:11-12

Remember, the word "corrupt," as we've seen it used in Scripture, means "moral perversion" and refers to meat or fruit that has become rotten or spoiled. The word *pervert* means "to become its opposite." To pervert is to do what Isaiah 5:20 says about calling evil good, and good evil. As we examine the time of the signs, we should be looking for people to use words and ideas in ways that are the opposite of what they used to mean and be. That will be part of the corruption that fills the earth in the last days.

The apostle Paul describes such corruption in the first chapter of Romans:

> Even as they did not like to retain God in their knowledge, God gave them over to a debased mind, to do those things which are not fitting; being filled with all unrighteousness, sexual immorality, wickedness, covetousness, maliciousness; full of envy, murder, strife, deceit, evil-mindedness; they are whisperers, backbiters, haters of God, violent, proud, boasters, inventors of evil things, disobedient to parents, undiscerning, untrustworthy, unloving, unforgiving, unmerciful; who, knowing the righteous judgment of God, that those who practice such things are deserving of death, not only do the same but also approve of those who practice them.

ROMANS 1:28-32

Our world has become the opposite of what it used to be. The moral and character flaws that are listed in Romans 1:28-32 have always been part of life in a fallen world, but there has long been a clearly defined line between good and evil. Even during the periods of history when evil seemed to be dominant and tyrants were brutal in their rule, people knew the difference between right and wrong, and good and evil. Good was still good, and evil was still evil. Yet Paul says in Romans 1 that when a nation (or the world) rejects God's existence and authority, a moral perversion will spread and lead to a time when the moral and character flaws in Romans 1:28-32 will become dominant. Paul closes this passage with what we could call the end of the digression and the point of no return. Society will have hit rock bottom, so to speak. He says in verse 32 that not only will moral perversion be practiced, it will be approved of.

I believe that one of the most significant signs of the last days is recorded here in Romans 1:32 even though the context of Paul's statement is general and not specific to eschatology. The word "approve" is the reason for this belief. "Approve" means "to feel good about, to be pleased with, to consent, agree to or applaud." That's how people will feel about the practices listed in Romans 1:28-31.

We could summarize Paul's conclusion by saying that *in the last days, moral depravity will become a human right.*

I need only mention two examples to confirm this is happening: women's rights marches and gay pride parades. We have all seen footage of the hundreds of thousands of women and men marching in women's rights marches. The "right" they are marching for is to legally kill an unborn child if they so choose—a moral depravity. In doing this, they outright reject long-recognized facts. The baby inside of the mother's womb is a separate individual with its own DNA, with genetic contributions from both mother and father. The baby is *not* part of the mother's body; he or she is an individual human being that, when left to the normal processes, will arrive into the world having features of both genetic contributors yet being distinct in their own way from them both. These facts are contrary to the unscientific mantra "My body, my choice."

When I was a boy growing up in Southern California, life was far different than it is now. On Sunday morning, churches were full and the local parks were empty. I remember when those who did not attend church were respectful of those who did. Today the parks are full of soccer, baseball, and football games, and church attendance is determined by sports schedules or personal plans that will allow for it. And the unchurched are not as respectful as they used to be about the churched.

In the past, homosexuality was not a topic of discussion in the way it is today. There was a season of time when, as things began to change, that we heard about people coming out of the closet, announcing that they were gay. In a single generation, this has transitioned to marching in pride parades on city streets. It's gotten to the point where grown men march naked in front of young children while their parents cheer and wave rainbow flags. The sad reality of how far our culture has fallen is revealed by the fact that a person who would normally be arrested for exposing themselves to a child isn't apprehended because the context is a gay parade.

Today, we not only have people who practice the kinds of behaviors described in Romans 1:28-31, but others who openly approve of and support them. Morally, people are the opposite of what they used to be. The world has become corrupt before God, just as it was in the days of Noah.

One last sign to consider as it relates to the world during the time of the signs: You may have seen cars with bumper stickers on them with the word *COEXIST*. There is a subtle though clear message tucked away behind this single word. The message is that religion is the problem behind many or even all of the world's problems. We're told that if religious groups could just "celebrate the common ground" between them and tolerate their differences, the world would be a better place. Sadly, the *T* in *COEXIST* is in the form of the cross, and thus Christianity is lumped together with some other religions represented by symbols that coincide with the other letters in the word. The Christian message of "love your enemies and do good to those who hate you" is lumped in with other religions, including one that has been known for religious extremism since its inception. While all religions have their extremists, Islam is more known for adherents that exhibit extremist behavior than other groups.

For those who might be thinking, *What about the Christian Crusades?*, a short run through history will remind us the Crusaders were taking back cities and countries taken by force from them by the Muslims. That didn't justify their behavior, but that was their motivation.

The spiritual basis behind the trend to get religious groups to set aside their differences is to prepare the world for the religion of beast worship that arises during the tribulation, which we see described in Revelation 13:

> They worshiped the dragon who gave authority to the beast; and they worshiped the beast, saying, "Who is like the beast? Who is able to make war with him?" And he was given a mouth speaking great things and blasphemies, and he was given authority to continue for forty-two months. Then he opened his mouth in blasphemy against God, to blaspheme His name, His tabernacle, and those who dwell in heaven. It was granted to him to make war with the saints and to overcome them. And authority was given him over every tribe, tongue, and nation. All who dwell on the earth will worship him, whose names have not been written in the Book of Life of the Lamb slain from the foundation of the world.
>
> **REVELATION 13:4-8**

The world is fast moving toward pushing for the extinction of the one true "religion of peace" due to Christianity's claim to be the only path to heaven and its moral code, which runs contrary to the flow of popular thought. To see just how delusional our world has become, consider the way that many politicians and world leaders are protecting and even promoting the practice of Islam, which refuses to submit to non-Muslim governmental systems and is not simply a religion but a political system as well and promotes Sharia law. Yet Western society blindly demands the coexistence of all belief systems while pushing for the extinction of the one that stands for truth, the Christian faith.

Western society blindly demands the coexistence of all belief systems while pushing for the extinction of the one that stands for truth, the Christian faith.

The world is readying itself for the ministry of the false prophet and his global religious system. The pump is being primed by people's demands that all religions be viewed as equal and that adherents of every religion respect the beliefs of others. This will never happen, and the only solution is for people to develop a one-world religion. The world is making itself ready for the greatest deception in all of human history: the pseudo-peace that will be offered to the world through the worship of the antichrist.

While it is clear that today's growing call for religious ecumenism is setting the stage for a one-world religion, what is often overlooked is the nature of that final global religion. It will not be Catholicism blended with Islam blended with Buddhism, like many have purported. Revelation 13 makes it clear that the global religion of the tribulation will be Satan worship. Everyone whose name is not written in the Lamb's Book of Life will worship the dragon who empowers and gives global authority to the beast. Imagine a world filled with Satan worshippers, and you can easily arrive at an understanding of why the tribulation saints will be hated to the degree that people prefer to see them dead. After all, their "god" only comes to steal, to kill, and to destroy (John 10:10).

The growing hatred of all things Christian and the rejection of the Judeo-Christian values that have long been the standard for defining morality tell us that our world is well on its way to the worship of the dragon and the first beast, as prophesied in Revelation 13. Remember, *worship* means "to prostrate and submit," and our world is now bowing before and submitting to things never dreamed of less than a quarter of a century ago.

These are just a few of the many developments that will take place on the world stage during the time of the signs. However, the church is not absent of signs happening within it that indicate the Day of the Lord is at hand. We will examine some of those next.

CHAPTER 4

SIGNS IN THE CHURCH

One fact the Bible makes clear about the last days is that within what is called the church, there will be a rejection of sound doctrine, which will lead to a defection from the faith. Faith, in this context, refers to the defining principles and precepts of Christianity. Paul seemed to be greatly troubled by this, because he warned of this frequently when he wrote to the churches.

> Let no one deceive you by any means; for that Day will not come unless the falling away comes first, and the man of sin is revealed, the son of perdition, who opposes and exalts himself above all that is called God or that is worshiped, so that he sits as God in the temple of God, showing himself that he is God.
>
> 2 THESSALONIANS 2:3-4

"That Day" Paul refers to is twofold. It speaks of the appearing of the Lord Jesus to gather His people to be with Him, or the rapture. It also refers to the second coming of Christ to the earth with His church. Both are aspects of the seventieth week of Daniel—the rapture precedes it, and the second coming concludes it. The phrase "falling away" is the Greek word *apostasia*, which is defined as "defection from truth." Another form of the word means "divorce, repudiation."

There is a generation of church history in which many people will defect from the truth and repudiate—or refuse to accept—all or part of the Word of God and divorce themselves from long-held teachings and moral statutes upheld by the church. It is important to note that here, the "church" is not a reference to true believers, but rather, to a group that Jesus referred to that includes "tares among the wheat" (Matthew 13:25). This same generation of church history will define truth by what is believed rather than letting truth define what is believed.

> Now the Spirit expressly says that in latter times some will depart from the faith, giving heed to deceiving spirits and doctrines of demons, speaking lies in hypocrisy, having their own conscience seared with a hot iron.
>
> 1 TIMOTHY 4:1-2

What a chilling statement! It implies that someday, what is called the church will not be the church at all (that is, the bride of Christ). It is worth noting that this is the only use in the Bible of the Greek word translated "expressly." It means "outspokenly" or "distinctly." This tells us that there is something specific about the latter times that is distinct from previous generations of church history. The distinguishing features of this time period will be departing from the faith, heeding spiritual deception, and teaching "doctrines of demons."

The word "conscience" speaks of moral convictions. Paul says that in the latter times, spiritual discernment will be so lacking in much of the church that doctrines of demons will not just go unrecognized, but will be taught, defended, and promoted as valid.

Another set of verses that can help us understand our topic for this chapter will require a bit of interpretive setup. There are varied opinions concerning the letters to the seven churches in Revelation chapters 2 and 3. Some believe these churches are presented in chronological order and represent churches through successive stages of church history. Others say all seven types of churches are present at all times in church history. I would agree that the primary context and content of these chapters had the seven literal churches in Asia Minor in mind, and that seven types of churches have been present at all times through church history. I would also say that the historical parallels to churches through the ages are undeniable, and thus like any letter penned by Paul, James, Peter, Luke, or John, the letters from Jesus to the churches have been applicable to all churches in every church age. This includes both the warnings and encouragements in the letters.

In the latter times, spiritual discernment will be
so lacking in much of the church that doctrines
of demons will not just go unrecognized, but will
be taught, defended, and promoted as valid.

With that in mind, consider that the last of the seven letters in Revelation 2–3 would represent the "latter times" Paul wrote about to Timothy. In that letter, we read:

> To the angel of the church of the Laodiceans write, "These things says the Amen, the Faithful and True Witness, the Beginning of the creation of God: 'I know your works, that you are neither cold nor hot. I could wish you were cold or hot. So then, because you are lukewarm, and neither cold nor hot, I will vomit you out of My mouth. Because

you say, "I am rich, have become wealthy, and have need of nothing"—and do not know that you are wretched, miserable, poor, blind, and naked—I counsel you to buy from Me gold refined in the fire, that you may be rich; and white garments, that you may be clothed, that the shame of your nakedness may not be revealed; and anoint your eyes with eye salve, that you may see.'"

REVELATION 3:14-18

One of the reasons we can see a chronology of church history within the seven letters is the parallels between the Laodicean letter and what Paul wrote in 1 Timothy 4:1-2. In both places, we find a season of church history identified, a departure from the faith recognized, demonic doctrine emphasized, and ignorant indifference actualized.

Also, the word *Laodicea* is a compound of *laos*, meaning "people," and *dikea*, meaning "judgment" or "rule," and Paul prophesied of such a generation of church history when he wrote his second letter to Timothy.

I charge you therefore before God and the Lord Jesus Christ, who will judge the living and the dead at His appearing and His kingdom: Preach the word! Be ready in season and out of season. Convince, rebuke, exhort, with all longsuffering and teaching. For the time will come when they will not endure sound doctrine, but according to their own desires, because they have itching ears, they will heap up for themselves teachers; and they will turn their ears away from the truth, and be turned aside to fables.

2 TIMOTHY 4:1-4

In the final season of church history before the rapture, many in the church will be teaching what people want to hear rather than what the Bible says. Like those in the church at Laodicea, people will rule in the sense that they dictate what is taught. They will be intolerant of sound teaching and prefer instructions that tickle the ears. They will use Christian terminology to fabricate lies and deceive others. They will depart from the faith and "heap up for themselves" teachers of fables. They will reject sound doctrine and allow for the rise of doctrines of demons. This will lead to the ignorant indifference Paul wrote of that will become dominant right before the Lord's appearing and the tribulation.

When I teach through the letters to the seven churches of Revelation 2 and 3, I like to point out that through the lens of a chronology of church history, there is no eighth letter. That means that in the latter times, when the apostasy is in full swing and doctrines of demons are preferred over the sound doctrines of the apostles, we will have reached the end of the church age and Jesus is coming soon.

If we consider the various scriptures that tell us of the spiritual state of what is called "the church" in the last days, we will find that they all have a common thread: They speak of a defection from long-held biblical truths. Today, these truths are being replaced with culturally sensitive messages that leave the listener feeling better about their fallen condition, with no unction in their spirits to repent or change their ways.

One of the primary points for us to consider about what will develop in the church during the time of the signs is this: *In the last days, church will become an activity rather than an identity.*

Today...truths are being replaced with culturally sensitive messages that leave the listener feeling better about their fallen condition.

When it comes to the last days, we can no longer limit our understanding of the word *church* to mean born-again believers. Yes, the church is made up of people, but these days, it's not just people who congregate on Sundays in a building set aside for the purpose of having a church service. Much of what is called "church" today is often what pastor Vance Havner described as the "Old Adam Improvement Society."[1] What he meant is that some churches have become places where the messages are crafted to increase people's "life experience" with little regard, if any, for the condition of the souls in attendance.

Looking back to what Paul wrote in 1 Timothy 4:1-2, note that he used the word "depart." The Greek word means "to instigate a revolt," or it can mean "to remove and withdraw." Thus, what Paul wrote in 1 Timothy 4, combined with what Jesus said to the church at Laodicea, should stand as a reminder and warning to us that the introduction of deception results in the exit of sound doctrine.

Deception was the first of the signs Jesus mentioned when He was asked about the sign of His coming:

> Now as He sat on the Mount of Olives, the disciples came to Him privately, saying, "Tell us, when will these things be? And what will be the sign of Your coming, and of the end of the age?" And Jesus answered and said to them: "Take heed that no one deceives you. For many will come in My name, saying, 'I am the Christ,' and will deceive many."
>
> MATTHEW 24:3-5

Most of the individuals who claim to be the second coming or reappearance of Jesus of Nazareth are quickly dismissed as frauds except by a relatively few confused followers. Our understanding of what Jesus was saying here in verse 4 is helped by remembering that Christ is referring to those who claim to be "anointed." During the time of the signs, there will be many who claim an anointing in the name of Jesus, and these deceivers will instigate a revolt against sound doctrine.

While there have always been defectors from truth in the church, the fact that this occurs in the context of the last days tells us that the problem will rise to the next level during that specific time period.

The danger that this poses during the last days is made clear when we consider what Paul wrote to the Romans: "So then faith comes by hearing, and hearing by the word of God" (Romans 10:17).

Claims of an anointing in the name of Jesus will be rampant in the last days. With that will come a shunning of sound doctrine that leaves those in the "church" unaware of the life-saving and eternal destiny-changing power of the gospel. Teachers will convince people that they are saved even though they have never heard the Word of God, but rather, fables about their destiny in this world. Teachers will encourage people to pursue what the Bible tells us to shun.

So how are we to respond to all this? James 1:21 urges us, "Therefore lay aside all filthiness and overflow of wickedness, and receive with meekness the implanted word, which is able to save your souls." To lay aside all filthiness and wickedness is to repent from sin. Repentance is a core doctrine of the Christian faith, and this is one of the doctrines that people will not endure during the time of the signs. Some call this easy believe-ism; others would label this phenomenon hyper grace, and still others would go so far as to say this kind of thinking promotes the universal salvation of all. But they all share in common the view that repentance is an outdated concept that the church needs to rethink. While these false teachers proclaim that salvation is possible for anyone, which is true, they also claim that repentance is necessary for no one, which is not true.

Paul wrote, "Now I plead with you, brethren, by the name of our Lord Jesus Christ, that you all speak the same thing, and that there be no divisions among you, but that you be perfectly joined together in the same mind and in the same judgment" (1 Corinthians 1:10). A cut-and-paste approach to teaching the Bible and the acceptance of doctrines of demons has become so commonplace today that when many people hear a message in church that is either convicting or counter to what is culturally acceptable, they don't change their ways; rather, they just change churches. This is why Paul stressed the importance of doctrinal unity, including our definitions of right and wrong. We see in the postmodern church the effort to eliminate any teaching that makes people uncomfortable or that would identify the church as being morally and spiritually distinct from the world. What's bizarre about this tactic is the Bible clearly says that the ministry of the Holy Spirit is to convict the world of sin (John 16:8), and that the church is to separate itself morally and spiritually from the things of the world (2 Corinthians 6:17).

This reminds me of the story of a man who had been shipwrecked on an island for many years. He was finally discovered by people on a passing ship, who saw his signal fire on the island. When the rescuers reached the shore, they found the man and noticed three huts on the beach. They asked, "How many others are here?" The man said, "It's just me." One of the rescuers asked, "Then why the three huts?" The man said, "The one on the left is my house, and the one in the middle is my church." The rescuers then asked, "What is the third hut?" The man said, "Oh, that's the church I used to go to."

Paul said that in the last days, many people will attend churches that tell them what they want to hear. People will want messages that make them comfortable and leave them just as they are. Anytime secularism creeps into a church, the Word of God goes out. Attendance might increase, but that doesn't mean the church has grown. When a spiritual vacuum is created by the absence of sound doctrine, Satan is more than willing to fill the void with deceiving spirits and doctrines of demons.

We would do well to remember what Jesus said in conclusion of the Sermon on the Mount.

Not everyone who says to Me, "Lord, Lord," shall enter the kingdom of heaven, but he who does the will of My Father in heaven. Many will say to Me in that day, "Lord, Lord, have we not prophesied in Your name, cast out demons in Your name, and done many wonders in Your name?" And then I will declare to them, "I never knew you; depart from Me, you who practice lawlessness!"

MATTHEW 7:21-23

The word "lawlessness" comes from the Greek word *anomia*. It means "to be without law." It does not mean to be aware of the law and disregard it, nor does it refer to the state of living with reckless disregard for the law, like some criminals do. It simply means to live as though there is no law to violate. Here, we need to pause and recognize the distinction between the law Jesus spoke of and the 613 ceremonial laws and customs given to the Jews via Moses (the Mosaic law). The law of Moses is not the law Jesus is referring to. That's because the law had no provision within it to save the human soul. Rather, it monitored outward behavior and observances. Paul went as far to say the law kills (see 2 Corinthians 3:6). We cannot be saved by keeping it (see Romans 7:11).

One of the deceiving doctrines taught today has to do with what is called hyper grace, or free grace. Its proponents believe that grace removes any moral standard by which Christians should live, thus denying repentance as a necessary part of being saved by grace through faith. Another term for this view is antinomianism—*anti* means "against," and *nomia* means "law" (as we saw a moment ago, *anomia* means "no law"). One tenet of free grace is that God is never upset or displeased with any of His children when they sin. You're going to have a hard time selling that idea to Ananias and Sapphira, who died because they had lied to God (Acts 5:1-10). And what do we do with the following admonishment?

You have forgotten the exhortation which speaks to you as to sons: "My son, do not despise the chastening of the LORD, nor be discouraged when you are rebuked by Him; for whom the LORD loves He chastens, and scourges every son whom He receives." If you endure chastening, God deals with you as with sons; for what son is there whom a father does not chasten? But if you are without chastening, of which all have become partakers, then you are illegitimate and not sons. Furthermore, we have had human fathers who corrected us, and we paid them respect. Shall we not much more readily be in subjection to the Father of spirits and live?

HEBREWS 12:5-9

If God is never upset with us when we do wrong, then what is the standard He uses to discipline us? Do we each just have our turn, or does God simply pick someone at random and say, "I think I'll chasten so and so today for no reason?" Hebrews 12:9 uses the word "corrected," which implies error, and error requires a standard that errors are measured against. That standard is not the 613 statutes of the Mosaic law; the standard is the universal moral code we call the Ten Commandments. Some would argue the Ten Commandments are for the Jews, yet none of them are related to religious observances. All of them have to do with our relationships with God and each other. If God is unchanging, then His moral code is unchanging. His standards in the Ten Commandments apply to all time.

Note what Jesus had to say on this matter:

Then one of them, a lawyer, asked Him a question, testing Him, and saying, "Teacher, which is the great commandment in the law?" Jesus said to him, "'You shall love the LORD your God with all your heart, with all your soul, and with all your mind.' This is the first and great commandment. And the second is like it: 'You shall love your neighbor as yourself.' On these two commandments hang all the Law and the Prophets."

MATTHEW 22:35-40

Jesus said loving God and loving our neighbor as ourselves summarizes the law of God. The first four commandments tell us how to love God, and the last six how to love others. To say there is no law is not an interpretation of Scripture, it is a doctrine of demons because it denies God's judicial nature, and because it nullifies His directive for us to be holy, thus making His discipline of us unjust.

Note what Paul commands of us in the book of Romans:

> I beseech you therefore, brethren, by the mercies of God, that you present your bodies a living sacrifice, holy, acceptable to God, which is your reasonable service. And do not be conformed to this world, but be transformed by the renewing of your mind, that you may prove what is that good and acceptable and perfect will of God.

ROMANS 12:1-2

You cannot prove the good and acceptable and perfect will of God through a life that looks no different than it did before you came to know Christ. Unfortunately, many people today view holiness, or moral purity, as a work, as though a person is trying to earn their salvation by being good. A phrase has even been coined for this—some people say that those who call for repentance and purity are teaching a "behavior modification gospel." The truth, however, is that knowing God changes us. It translates us from the kingdom of darkness into His glorious light. It modifies our behavior from that of a lover of darkness to one who walks in the light.

In an age where many in the church argue that God is love and love never condemns, and a God of love would never send anyone to hell, we need to remember this: In all of the Bible, there are only two times that we are told that God is love. However, there are more than 400 times when we are told that God is holy. And as children of God, we are called to be holy as well:

> Gird up the loins of your mind, be sober, and rest your hope fully upon the grace that is to be brought to you at the revelation of Jesus Christ; as obedient children, not conforming yourselves to the former lusts, as in your ignorance; but as He who called you is holy, you also be holy in all your conduct, because it is written, "Be holy, for I am holy."
>
> 1 PETER 1:13-16

Those who decry any mention of repentance as a necessary evidence of salvation take the position that the believer's holiness is merely positional. Because we are in Christ and Christ is holy, so we are holy. Yet Peter, who knew Christ in ways we have yet to experience, said holiness is also practical and is to be manifest in all our conduct. Some people argue that being saved by grace through faith denies any need for change in the life of a believer because salvation is "not of works, lest anyone should boast" (Ephesians 2:8-10). The problem with this thinking is that holiness is not works; rather, holiness has to do with reflecting God in our everyday lives by living in a manner that is morally pure.

Also, the hyper grace crowd needs to remember that grace is God's *method*, not God's *message*. And the apostle John makes it clear that to walk in the light is to practice the truth.

> This is the message which we have heard from Him and declare to you, that God is light and in Him is no darkness

at all. If we say that we have fellowship with Him, and walk in darkness, we lie and do not practice the truth. But if we walk in the light as He is in the light, we have fellowship with one another, and the blood of Jesus Christ His Son cleanses us from all sin.

1 JOHN 1:5-7

One of the other defections from truth we are seeing in these last days is the prosperity gospel. Those who teach this gospel claim that sickness or physical weakness can be displaced from our lives by faith. They say that if we are weak or sick, it is because of a lapse of faith. This teaching is paired with the claim that we can declare wealth into our life, and that if we are poor, it is because we lack faith.

There is another word for believing you can actualize your own reality of health and prosperity—that word is *magic*. Believing that you can improve your life experience by increasing your faith is an antibiblical teaching from the Word of Faith movement.

In contrast to the kind of thinking promoted by Word of Faith teaching, Paul wrote this:

Not that I speak in regard to need, for I have learned in whatever state I am, to be content: I know how to be abased, and I know how to abound. Everywhere and in all things I have learned both to be full and to be hungry, both to abound and to suffer need. I can do all things through Christ who strengthens me.

PHILIPPIANS 4:11-13

Paul said that part of his Christian experience was being abased, which means to live in humble circumstances. He said his Christian life by faith included being hungry and suffering need. He also experienced the opposite, but his point here is that God always supplied him with the strength to do all things through Christ no matter what his social or financial status. Living in humble circumstances, being hungry, and suffering need did not result from lapses of faith. Rather, such circumstances called for him to employ his faith.

Christians suffer lean times and experience good times. They get sick and enjoy times of health. They have times of need and times of abundance. Whatever you are experiencing right now is the end result of living in a fallen world—it's not because you don't have enough faith. Consider these words from Paul:

> Lest I should be exalted above measure by the abundance of the revelations, a thorn in the flesh was given to me, a messenger of Satan to buffet me, lest I be exalted above measure. Concerning this thing I pleaded with the Lord three times that it might depart from me. And He said to me, "My grace is sufficient for you, for My strength is made perfect in weakness." Therefore most gladly I will rather boast in my infirmities, that the power of Christ may rest upon me. Therefore I take pleasure in infirmities, in reproaches, in needs, in persecutions, in distresses, for Christ's sake. For when I am weak, then I am strong.
>
> 2 CORINTHIANS 12:7-10

There are some who believe, because of a comment made in Galatians 4:15 about the Galatians being willing to pluck out their eyes and give them to Paul, if that were possible, that Paul suffered one of the many eye ailments that were common during the first century AD. Some have speculated it was ophthalmia, an eye inflammation that caused an ugly discharge and poor vision. While that is a possibility, that is not the point here. The lesson is that Paul, a great man of faith, pleaded with the Lord for healing, and the Lord said, "No. My grace is sufficient for you."

According to the Word of Faith movement, this passage cannot be true. They say that faith enables us to actualize our own healthy and prosperous reality. They say that because the object of our faith is God, and because it is He who has given us faith, then Paul should have been able to decree his own healing. But he didn't, and he couldn't, because that is not what faith is. Hebrews 11:1 defines faith this way: "Now faith is the substance of things hoped for, the evidence of things not seen."

Faith is most tangible to others when they see us trusting God through the same things that often cause the unsaved to panic or fall into despair. Faith is what makes our belief visible to others. God is not anti-material; He blessed Abraham, David, and Solomon with great riches. But none of them sought their wealth or asked for it.

> Faith is most tangible to others when they see us trusting God through the same things that often cause the unsaved to panic or fall into despair.

In the time of the signs, there will be a radical shift in the thinking and beliefs of the "church," resulting in the church modeling itself after the world rather than following the historical beliefs of the Christian faith. Yet Peter and John, who heard Jesus with their own ears and saw Him with their own eyes, both reported on His teaching and concluded that being a Christian is a way of life modeled after Christ Himself. It is walking in the light and holiness, and not in darkness and moral impurity. A Christian pursues the things of God, not the things of this world, which are passing away.

We are living in the last age of church history and the parallels between the church at Laodicea and the postmodern church are undeniable. Errant perspectives on self, spiritual blindness, and a focus on personal prosperity all reveal the defection from truth that is expected in the time of the signs. Repentance is unpopular and deemed unnecessary. Sexual behaviors outside of biblical parameters are culturally accepted, and there are many churches that accept those behaviors too. We live in an age in which churches are ruled by people's wishes and demands, which indicates the defection from truth is in full swing.

Our conclusion, therefore, must be that Jesus is coming for us soon!

CHAPTER 5

THE RAPTURE

As we consider the ways that the church has indulged in self-rule and a wholesale rejection of what makes the church what it is supposed to be, we need to keep in mind what Jesus said about the believer's responsibility and calling in this dark and delusional world.

> You are the salt of the earth; but if the salt loses its flavor, how shall it be seasoned? It is then good for nothing but to be thrown out and trampled underfoot by men. You are the light of the world. A city that is set on a hill cannot be hidden. Nor do they light a lamp and put it under a basket, but on a lampstand, and it gives light to all who are in the house. Let your light so shine before men, that they may see your good works and glorify your Father in heaven.
>
> **MATTHEW 5:13-16**

When good works are viewed as imposing on being saved by grace, and when the light has largely gone out in the church (with light being representative of truth), then the end result is that the church is overrun by the world and trampled underfoot by men. When this happens, the Lord is no longer able to use the church to receive glory for the good work of "truth bearing" to a lost and dying world. While Jesus' statements in the Sermon on the Mount are not related to the time of the signs, they do make a relevant point. When the church no longer has a purifying and preserving influence on the world, and it is no longer bringing glory to God, then it seems safe to say the timing is right for the world to transition back to the 70 weeks of Daniel and to experience the fulfillment of the seventieth and final week, or the tribulation.

While the rapture of the church is taught as being imminent and the day and hour are unknown, there are many clues that tell us this event is imminent. Among these clues is the rebirth of the nation of Israel. Because the purpose of the regathering of the Jewish people is to fulfill prophecy and complete the discipline of God's chosen people, and because the church has no part in the seventieth week of Daniel, we can assume the rapture is getting closer.

We do not know the day or hour of the glorious appearing of our great God and Savior Jesus Christ. But we do know that the purpose of the regathering of the Jews in their covenantal homeland is for God to afflict them and cause a believing remnant (Zechariah 12:10) to recognize the error of rejecting Christ. As Hosea 5:15 says, the Jews' affliction will cause them to receive the Lord: "They will seek My face; in their affliction they will earnestly seek Me."

The first and obvious thing for us to recognize is that for "all Israel [to] be saved" (Romans 11:26), there has to be an Israel. The fact that the nation exists today is not just happenstance or a prophetically irrelevant reality. It is a miraculous fulfillment of multiple prophecies.

The whole tribulation is a time of God's wrath (more on that in the next chapter), and the church does not have an appointment with it. As 1 Thessalonians 5:9 says, "God did not appoint us to wrath, but to obtain salvation through our Lord Jesus Christ." This necessitates the removal of the church before the tribulation, and Jesus directly promised this in the sixth letter of the seven He sent to the churches of Asia Minor in Revelation 2–3:

> Because you have kept My command to persevere, I also will keep you from the hour of trial which shall come upon the whole world, to test those who dwell on the earth.

REVELATION 3:10

The Greek preposition ἐκ, translated "from," can also be translated "out of." This eliminates the possibility of interpreting this as saying Jesus promised to keep the church "through" the tribulation, which is what will happen to the Jews who later look upon Him whom they pierced and mourn (Zechariah 12:10). The church will be kept out of the entire seven-year tribulation, not protected through it. What is the point of the church going through the tribulation and being protected during it? What benefit is there for the church to go through it yet not be impacted by it? Are we to be observers? Scripture does not mention the church as being among those who are witnesses during the tribulation, like the 144,000. It is not necessary for the church to go through this time to be purified, for to say that means the blood of Christ was not a sufficient sacrifice to cover our sins. To hold the view that the church will go through the tribulation is to say we are saved by grace *and* tribulation, or we are purified by trial.

None of that is true or biblically feasible!

Here's another reason we can assume the rapture is getting close—while it is a bit speculative, it makes logical sense. If the church has largely ceased being a purifying influence in the world (being salt) and has replaced the light of God's truth with doctrines of demons and socially acceptable ideas, then what is the point of having the church remain on earth during the tribulation? Again, this is speculation, but it makes sense. The Jews are back in their national homeland, and the church has largely defected from the truth (though a faithful remnant remains). Thus, for the rapture to happen soon seems likely. We also need to remember that the day and hour has already been determined. The trends we just talked about won't cause the rapture, they are simply signs that indicate it is likely near.

Sadly, the truth that the church will be raptured has become a divisive subject in these last days instead of a glorious expectation. Some argue that the Bible presents no such doctrine, while others debate its timing. There are many today who view the subject of the rapture as *inciting* rather than *exciting*. They say inciting in the sense it elicits cries of heresy and sensationalism or escapism from a growing number of saints today.

In response to the growing number of people who deny the presence of the rapture in Scripture, we need to address the issue for two reasons and from two perspectives: proper hermeneutics and accurate eschatology. I would hazard a guess that because you are reading this book, you have an interest in Bible prophecy, and you likely have views about this hotly debated topic. In this chapter, we are going to answer these questions: What is the timing of the rapture in terms of the end-times chronology? And, can the rapture be defended biblically?

Hermeneutics is simply a fancy word for interpretation, and here's our hermeneutical question: Does the Bible actually teach the rapture? The short answer is yes. And because the Bible clearly teaches the rapture, let's review all the verses in which the word *rapture* is used so we can arrive at an accurate eschatology. Yet there aren't any instances of the word *rapture* in Scripture, are there? Then how can a doctrine be valid when the word isn't even used?

Let's use that argument to make a point. We don't find the word *rapture* in our English Bibles. Are there any other major doctrines that we believe that aren't described by a specific word in the Bible? Yes—the Trinity or triunity of God is one example. The doctrine of the Trinity is an essential that cannot be denied without compromising the principles of saving faith.

One passage that affirms the doctrine of the Trinity has to do with Jesus' baptism.

> It came to pass in those days that Jesus came from Nazareth of Galilee, and was baptized by John in the Jordan. And immediately, coming up from the water, He saw the heavens parting and the Spirit descending upon Him like a dove. Then a voice came from heaven, "You are My beloved Son, in whom I am well pleased."
>
> **MARK 1:9-11**

We find in this scene the three distinct personages of the one eternal God, and yet the terms *Trinity* or *triunity* are not used. Still, all three members of the triune Godhead are simultaneously present.

We also find the Trinity mentioned in the creation narrative in Genesis: "In the beginning God created the heavens and the earth. The earth was without form, and void; and darkness was on the face of the deep. And the Spirit of God was hovering over the face of the waters" (Genesis 1:1-2).

The word translated "God" is the Hebrew term *Elohim,* and it speaks of the plurality of God—not multiple Gods, but the one God manifested in a Trinity. The Father and the Spirit are present and active at creation, and then later in the narrative, we find the Son: "God said, 'Let Us make man in Our image, according to Our likeness; let them have dominion over the fish of the sea, over the birds of the air, and over the cattle, over all the earth and over every creeping thing that creeps on the earth'" (verse 26).

Colossians 1:15-16 says that Jesus is the "image" of the invisible God, and that all things were created through and for Him. Though we find the invisible God, the Holy Spirit, and the physical manifestation of God in the person of Jesus in Genesis, we don't find the word *Trinity.*

So the argument that there is no such thing as the rapture because the word doesn't appear in our English Bibles is nullified by the precedent set by the word *Trinity*. The Trinity is clearly present in Genesis and is confirmed in the Gospels. Just because a word used to describe a doctrine or precept is not found in Scripture does not mean that doctrine or precept is invalid.

Another common objection is that the doctrine of the rapture arrived late in church history—it is not part of ancient or accurate eschatology. The problem with this thinking is that if we can find the doctrine mentioned in the Bible (even though the word *rapture* itself isn't used), then the doctrine of the rapture is as old as the Bible. There are three ways we can establish the rapture of the church as sound doctrine: Old Testament precedent or typology, New Testament clarity, and prophetic necessity. By prophetic necessity, I mean this: Does the absence of the doctrine of the rapture leave holes in the prophetic narrative or time line?

If we can establish these three points, then we can safely conclude the rapture is neither new nor a mere human invention. It is as sound a doctrine as any other in Scripture. Before we dig in and respond to the claim that the doctrine of the rapture is recent, let's start by looking at Daniel 12:4: "You, Daniel, shut up the words, and seal the book until the time of the end; many shall run to and fro, and knowledge shall increase."

This passage tells us that those living closer to the end times will have more prophetic clarity than those further away. This is problematic for those who say belief in the rapture is false based on its recent development and popularity. Scripture clearly says some elements of the last days scenario will become knowable only to those living in those days. Even so, the teaching that the church will experience a pre-tribulation rapture has a much deeper biblical base than some people are willing to acknowledge. Our goal, then, is to be Bereans, and put this doctrine to the test and see if it holds up.

On to our first criterion: Do we find Old Testament precedents or typologies that validate the rapture as a doctrine taught cover to cover in Scripture? In search of our answer, let's start with 1 Corinthians 15:

> Behold, I tell you a mystery: We shall not all sleep, but we shall all be changed—in a moment, in the twinkling of an eye, at the last trumpet. For the trumpet will sound, and the dead will be raised incorruptible, and we shall be changed.
>
> 1 CORINTHIANS 15:51-52

If you're thinking, *First Corinthians is in the New Testament*, keep reading! The Greek word for "mystery" is μυστήριον (*mysterion*), and it means "not obvious to the understanding." We will talk more about this verse in our second criterion, but the point here is that there are scriptural concepts in the Old Testament that were not obvious to the understanding of those who lived in the time of their writing, just as Daniel 12:4 states. For example: The full meanings of the statue in Daniel 2 and the four beasts in Daniel 7 were not obvious to readers when those passages were written. But as time marched on, the meaning of those passages became clearer. Now we can look back over history and see the successive world empires of the Babylonians, Medo-Persians, and the Greeks, who were named, and the Romans, who were not.

Can the mystery of the rapture be established by a foreshadowing of it in the Old Testament? First, we need to ask what exactly the rapture implies. As a doctrine, the rapture implies two things: an instantaneous translation of living human beings from this world to the next by means of a supernatural agent. And second, a separation of God's people from His direct wrath on His enemies.

Let's first look for Old Testament precedents for an instant translation from this life to the next. Here's one:

> Enoch lived sixty-five years, and begot Methuselah. After
> he begot Methuselah, Enoch walked with God three
> hundred years, and had sons and daughters. So all the
> days of Enoch were three hundred and sixty-five years.
> And Enoch walked with God; and he was not, for God
> took him.
>
> GENESIS 5:21-24

The word "took" is key. The Hebrew word means "to fetch or
catch away." The Greek word *harpazo*, translated as "caught up" in
1 Thessalonians 4:17, carries the same meaning: "to take up by force,
to snatch away."

Here's another Old Testament precedent:

> Then it happened, as they continued on and talked, that
> suddenly a chariot of fire appeared with horses of fire,
> and separated the two of them; and Elijah went up by a
> whirlwind into heaven.
>
> 2 KINGS 2:11

Based on our findings in the Old Testament, we can say the first
part of our criteria has been met. There is, in the Old Testament, a
precedent that validates the possibility of an instantaneous translation from this life to the next by means of a supernatural agent—the
translation of flesh-and-blood humans who pleased and served God.

There is another passage that helps us to refute any who would
argue there are no Old Testament typologies of the New Testament
rapture:

> They themselves declare concerning us what manner of
> entry we had to you, and how you turned to God from
> idols to serve the living and true God, and to wait for His

Son from heaven, whom He raised from the dead, even
Jesus who delivers us from the wrath to come.

1 THESSALONIANS 1:9-10

We will deal with other New Testament scriptures that teach about
our deliverance from God's direct wrath, but this will introduce the
concept for us. There are those who say the church will go through
the tribulation even as the saints of old have gone through tribulations. For support, they point to passages like John 16:33: "These
things I have spoken to you, that in Me you may have peace. In the
world you will have tribulation; but be of good cheer, I have overcome the world."

The word translated "tribulation" means "anguish, troubles, afflictions." There is nothing that implies these troubles are initiated by
the Lord or are a form of His wrath. Having tribulations in this life
does not mean we will go through the seven-year tribulation that is
clearly a time of God's wrath. In this life, we can expect troubling
things to happen that will cause anguish and afflictions. But Christ
has overcome this world, and these troubles are only temporary and
are a normal part of the Christian life. They are not specific to a
future seven-year time period.

Having tribulations in this life does not mean
we will go through the seven-year tribulation
that is clearly a time of God's wrath.

With regard to Old Testament types of deliverance from God's
wrath, we can note that Noah was delivered from God's wrath when
the ark lifted him above the waters of the flood. Lot was delivered

from God's judgment on Sodom and Gomorrah when he was removed from the area. The Israelites were delivered from God's wrath when the last seven plagues pounded the Egyptians into submission to God's will for His people. There are some who argue that the Israelites were still on the planet when God poured out His wrath on the Egyptians, and they use this to claim the typology states the church will go through the tribulation and God will supernaturally protect it.

But that reasoning doesn't hold up. Israel is Israel, and the church is the church. The church has not replaced Israel, and God is not finished with His people. The only principles relating to Israel that we can apply to the church are those pertaining to the nature and character of God. Now pay close attention: Neither Noah nor Lot were Jews. And God moved both of them to prevent them from exposure to His wrath. Noah was lifted above the waters; Lot was removed from Sodom.

Let's look next at what happened with Israel:

> In that day I will set apart the land of Goshen, in which My people dwell, that no swarms of flies shall be there, in order that you may know that I am the LORD in the midst of the land. I will make a difference between My people and your people. Tomorrow this sign shall be.
>
> EXODUS 8:22-23

Israel remained in Egypt, which is a type of the world, during the time of the ten plagues. But the Jewish people were supernaturally protected by God during the last seven plagues. How long is the tribulation? Seven years. So, too, will the Jewish people remain on the earth and be supernaturally protected throughout the time of God's wrath (more on that later).

However, Noah was removed from the flood when the door of the ark was shut by God. Lot was removed from wrath when the angels met him and led him out of Sodom. Therefore, in the cases of Noah and Lot, we have a supernatural agent and a change of location that delivered them from God's wrath. In Egypt, we have the divine protection of Jews during the time of God's wrath, just as will happen during the tribulation. Notice also that when the Lord spoke to Pharaoh, the separation of God's people from wrath was a sign to the world.

In these ways, Old Testament precedents for the rapture are clear and well defined.

What about New Testament clarity? Again, some say the word *rapture* isn't present in Scripture. How, then, is the mystery in the Old Testament made clear in the New? Are the words *gracias* or *bonjour* in the Bible? Yes, they are—just not in our English Bibles. Those words are translated "thanks" or "greetings."

So is the word *rapture* in the Bible? Let's take a closer look.

> This we say to you by the word of the Lord, that we who are alive and remain until the coming of the Lord will by no means precede those who are asleep. For the Lord Himself will descend from heaven with a shout, with the voice of an archangel, and with the trumpet of God. And the dead in Christ will rise first. Then we who are alive and remain shall be caught up together with them in the clouds to meet the Lord in the air. And thus we shall always be with the Lord.
>
> **1 THESSALONIANS 4:15-17**

The word translated as "caught up" is ἁρπάζω (*harpazo*). It means "to pluck, to pull, to catch up by force." If you have a Latin Bible, you would see the word *rapturos* instead of ἁρπάζω, so yes, the word *rapture* is in the Bible—just not our English versions.

Paul says that living believers will be caught up together with the dead saints to meet the Lord in the air and be with Him forever. They will experience an instantaneous translation from this life to the next via a supernatural agent. For us to live eternally will require that we have a body able to do that. The bodies we currently dwell in cannot. So, for us to have bodies meant to exist eternally, we have to be changed at the rapture, and indeed, that's what will happen.

> Behold, I tell you a mystery: We shall not all sleep, but we shall all be changed—in a moment, in the twinkling of an eye, at the last trumpet. For the trumpet will sound, and the dead will be raised incorruptible, and we shall be changed. For this corruptible must put on incorruption, and this mortal must put on immortality. So when this corruptible has put on incorruption, and this mortal has put on immortality, then shall be brought to pass the saying that is written: "Death is swallowed up in victory." "O Death, where is your sting? O Hades, where is your victory?"
>
> 1 CORINTHIANS 15:51-55

"Sleep" is an idiom for death, and Paul says we will not all die, but we will all be changed. Changed into what? Incorruptible, immortal beings capable of existing eternally. How quickly? In the twinkling of an eye. That is instantaneous! Where are we meeting the Lord? In the air. And how long will we be with Him? Forever. Will death continue to be a threat to us? No!

We have to ask: What would be the figurative meaning of such verses if there is no rapture? This can't be a picture of salvation because we don't get new bodies when we are saved. This can't speak of the soul because the soul never dies—it is already immortal. So, what can 1 Corinthians 15:51-55 mean? Let's look at some other passages for the answer.

> Our citizenship is in heaven, from which we also eagerly wait for the Savior, the Lord Jesus Christ, who will

transform our lowly body that it may be conformed to His glorious body, according to the working by which He is able even to subdue all things to Himself.

PHILIPPIANS 3:20-21

Paul said we will not all die, which has to pertain to the human body, not the human soul, which doesn't die. Our lowly and limited bodies are going to be transformed (also translated as transfigured) into their predestined form of the "image" (the Greek is εἰκών, *eikon*) of Christ.

> We know that the whole creation groans and labors with birth pangs together until now. Not only that, but we also who have the firstfruits of the Spirit, even we ourselves groan within ourselves, eagerly waiting for the adoption, the redemption of our body. For we were saved in this hope, but hope that is seen is not hope; for why does one still hope for what he sees? But if we hope for what we do not see, we eagerly wait for it with perseverance.

ROMANS 8:22-25

"Redemption" refers to a release effected by the payment of a ransom. We are waiting for our bodies to be redeemed after long having been confined to the expectancy of death. Romans 8 does not give details about the transition of our bodies into glorious ones like Christ's, but it does say that's what awaits us.

First Corinthians 15:52 tells us about the speed of the transition: in the twinkling of an eye. And Philippians further explains we will become immortal and incorruptible. Our destination is glorious, Christlike bodies. The New Testament is clear about the mystery in the Old: We will someday be translated into bodies that are capable of existing eternally. There is no mistaking this.

We have established Old Testament types and precedence, and we have New Testament clarity. What about prophetic necessity? Will there be holes left in the prophetic narrative if there is no rapture of the church? Must *all* of the Bible's prophecies come to pass for Scripture to be reliable and trustworthy? Can unconditional and eternal promises be forfeited or applied to another group of people in the Bible, and Scripture still be a source of immutable or unchanging truth? The answer is no, because what was once true must always be true.

Next, let's address the matter of the church and God's wrath, starting with this passage in Revelation:

> The kings of the earth, the great men, the rich men, the commanders, the mighty men, every slave and every free man, hid themselves in the caves and in the rocks of the mountains, and said to the mountains and rocks, "Fall on us and hide us from the face of Him who sits on the throne and from the wrath of the Lamb! For the great day of His wrath has come, and who is able to stand?"
>
> REVELATION 6:15-17

The word translated "every" in John's day meant "every." What does it mean today? "Every." In other words, rich or poor, slave or free, *every* person on the earth will try to hide from Him who sits on the throne and from the wrath of the Lamb. Absolutely no one will be able to stand. We do not find the phrase "except the church" present anywhere in the text; thus, the church cannot be a part of this scene and is not present on the earth at the time of this event.

Is there a biblical precedent in Scripture for the Lamb of God becoming a lion against His own bride and killing her along with evildoers without discrimination? Are there any times when the church has had to hide from God's wrath? The apostle Paul said no:

God did not appoint us to wrath, but to obtain salvation through our Lord Jesus Christ, who died for us, that whether we wake or sleep, we should live together with Him. Therefore comfort each other and edify one another, just as you also are doing.

1 THESSALONIANS 5:9-11

If the rapture is not a sound biblical doctrine, then there is a discrepancy between 1 Thessalonians 5:9-22 and Revelation 6:15-17, and that opens up a plethora of problems. The Bible would not be trustworthy if verses contradict one another.

Even in the early church, there were some who spread confusion about the rapture. In response, Paul wrote,

Now, brethren, concerning the coming of our Lord Jesus Christ and our gathering together to Him, we ask you, not to be soon shaken in mind or troubled, either by spirit or by word or by letter, as if from us, as though the day of Christ had come. Let no one deceive you by any means; for that Day will not come unless the falling away comes first, and the man of sin is revealed, the son of perdition, who opposes and exalts himself above all that is called God or that is worshiped, so that he sits as God in the temple of God, showing himself that he is God.

Do you not remember that when I was still with you I told you these things? And now you know what is restraining, that he may be revealed in his own time. For the mystery of lawlessness is already at work; only He who now restrains will do so until He is taken out of the way. And then the lawless one will be revealed, whom the Lord will

consume with the breath of His mouth and destroy with
the brightness of His coming.

2 THESSALONIANS 2:1-8

There are some who see the phrase "falling away" as a reference to
the rapture because the Greek word ἀποστασία, or *apostasia*, can be
translated "departure." The problem is that in Scripture, ἀποστασία
is never used in the context of a physical departure. It is always used
to refer to a departing from truth. The term is used only one other
time in the Bible, in Acts 21:21, and that context has the same meaning intended here: forsaking God's Word.

I believe the rapture is found here in the phrase "gathering together,"
which means "the complete assembly," or "to assemble in one place."
What is the end result of the rapture? The whole church is gathered
in once place. If ἀποστασία were pointing to the rapture, as some
say, and "gathering together" is pointing to the rapture, then this
text would say, "The rapture can't happen unless the rapture happens first." That is obviously redundant. Paul was saying, "Don't let
the words or letters of others shake you up with regard to what I've
taught about our gathering together to Him." We shouldn't let the
words of today's naysayers trouble us either.

The idea of being gathered together to Christ is consistent with
what Jesus said to the eleven on the night of His betrayal and arrest.
He said He was going to prepare a place for them, and that He would
come again and receive them unto Himself so that where He is, they
(and we) may be also (John 14:2-3).

What about the timing of the rapture? That's another hotly debated
subject in the church. While most acknowledge the day and hour is
unknowable, is that day and hour *before* the tribulation, *during* the
tribulation, or at the *end* of the tribulation? (These are the pre-, mid-,
and post-tribulation rapture views.) Does not knowing the day or
hour mean we can't know anything about the timing of the rapture in

relation to the tribulation? That depends on which timing view you hold to. If you believe in a pre-tribulation rapture, then seeing things develop that will be fulfilled during the tribulation should stir up a sense of expectation and excitement because it could happen at any time. But if you are mid- or post-trib, then you know that because the tribulation has not yet begun, there is no expectation that the rapture could occur within the next three-and-a-half or seven years.

Not only has there been significant debate about the timing of the rapture, there are some who reject the idea of a rapture altogether:

> Knowing this first: that scoffers will come in the last days, walking according to their own lusts, and saying, "Where is the promise of His coming? For since the fathers fell asleep, all things continue as they were from the beginning of creation." For this they willfully forget: that by the word of God the heavens were of old, and the earth standing out of water and in the water, by which the world that then existed perished, being flooded with water. But the heavens and the earth which are now preserved by the same word, are reserved for fire until the day of judgment and perdition of ungodly men.
>
> 2 PETER 3:3-7

Sadly, there are a multitude of "rapture scoffers" with us today who are fulfilling Peter's warning. This is also consistent with Jesus stating that He would come at a time when He was not expected (Matthew 24:44). If you don't believe in the rapture, you certainly aren't going to be expecting it.

In 2 Thessalonians 2, the next point Paul makes to the church is, "Let no one deceive you" about this (verse 3). Then he lists a progression of events that will initiate the march toward the destruction of the man of sin by the brightness of Jesus' second coming. Here is our point of interest: Lawlessness is already at work. That which is restraining the rise of the antichrist and his kingdom is going to be taken out of the way, and then—and *only* then—will the lawless one be revealed. What is the restraining force holding back utter lawlessness in the world today? The Holy Spirit. What is the dwelling place of the Holy Spirit? In the saints who make up the church.

That means that if the restraining force holding back the rise of the antichrist is the Holy Spirit, and if He dwells in the saints or the church, then the church must be taken out of the way for the lawless one to rise to power. If there is no rapture, then this progression doesn't make sense. For how can the world's only source of salt and light be present at a time when there is no restraining force on the earth?

This leads to another question: Can the true church be present on the earth and *not* be a restraining force by the power of the Holy Spirit? Can the true church cease from being salt and light? What is the solution to our question and prophetic dilemma? The rapture.

> Take heed to yourselves, lest your hearts be weighed down
> with carousing, drunkenness, and cares of this life, and
> that Day come on you unexpectedly. For it will come as
> a snare on all those who dwell on the face of the whole
> earth. Watch therefore, and pray always that you may be
> counted worthy to escape all these things that will come
> to pass, and to stand before the Son of Man.
>
> LUKE 21:34-36

The word "escape" means "to flee out of." Jesus described this time as one that no flesh would survive unless He did not return to stop it, and He warned that it would be a time of global judgment. Where, then, do hundreds of millions of Christians "flee out of" in order to escape that judgment? What do those verses mean if the church goes through the tribulation?

What about a mid-tribulation or pre-wrath rapture? These views say we will miss God's wrath and be here for the first half of the tribulation. Those positions conflict with what 2 Thessalonians 2 says about the church hindering the antichrist's rise to power, and the church's departure (the removal of the Holy Spirit) being the event that allows him to rise. The antichrist will be given power to reign during the first 42 months of the tribulation. We know this because the first of the four horsemen of the apocalypse in Revelation 6 is a man on a white horse who brings a pseudo-peace to the world through the seven-year covenant he establishes with Israel, as prophesied in Daniel 9:27.

In spite of scoffers and deniers, the doctrine of the rapture of the church is as sound as any other doctrine of Scripture. It is clear that God can protect the Jews from His wrath, and it is clear that on other occasions, He has changed the location of Gentiles to remove them from His wrath. The New Testament not only teaches the rapture, it requires it. The prophetic narrative and sequence of end-times events is completely disrupted without the supernatural removal of the church from the earth prior to the tribulation.

If we can see events that are exclusive to
the tribulation approaching, we can be
sure the rapture of the church is near!

No man knows the day or the hour of the Lord's coming for His church. But if we can see events that are exclusive to the tribulation approaching, we can be sure the rapture of the church is near! So what are some of the signs that indicate the tribulation is drawing closer?

CHAPTER 6

THE WAR
OF EZEKIEL

Before we examine specifics about the event recorded in Ezekiel 38–39, we need to establish the timing of this event and why it is likely a tribulation event, or at least part of it.

> "It will come to pass at the same time, when Gog comes against the land of Israel," says the Lord GOD, "that My fury will show in My face. For in My jealousy and in the fire of My wrath I have spoken: 'Surely in that day there shall be a great earthquake in the land of Israel, so that the fish of the sea, the birds of the heavens, the beasts of the field, all creeping things that creep on the earth, and all men who are on the face of the earth shall shake at My presence. The mountains shall be thrown down, the steep places shall fall, and every wall shall fall to the ground.' I will call for a sword against Gog throughout all My mountains," says the Lord GOD. "Every man's sword will be against his brother. And I will bring him to judgment with pestilence and bloodshed; I will rain down on him, on his troops, and on the many peoples

who are with him, flooding rain, great hailstones, fire, and brimstone."

EZEKIEL 38:18-22

Some argue that the war described here by Ezekiel is the famed Battle of Armageddon. Others say Ezekiel 38 and 39 record two different events. Some say Revelation 20 and Ezekiel 38 and 39 are talking about the same battle. We will deal with those varying interpretations shortly, but whatever one's interpretive position may be, there is evidence as to when the battle will end, and we'll examine that in a moment. First, let's consider who is involved.

Now the word of the LORD came to me, saying, "Son of man, set your face against Gog, of the land of Magog, the prince of Rosh, Meshech, and Tubal, and prophesy against him, and say, 'Thus says the Lord GOD: "Behold, I am against you, O Gog, the prince of Rosh, Meshech, and Tubal. I will turn you around, put hooks into your jaws, and lead you out, with all your army, horses, and horsemen, all splendidly clothed, a great company with bucklers and shields, all of them handling swords. Persia, Ethiopia, and Libya are with them, all of them with shield and helmet; Gomer and all its troops; the house of Togarmah from the far north and all its troops—many people are with you."'"

EZEKIEL 38:1-6

We can find references to most of the names here in Genesis 10, where the immediate descendants of Noah are mentioned. Absent from the list in Genesis 10 are Gog, Libya, Persia, Ethiopia, and Rosh. Magog, Meshech, Tubal, Gomer, and Togarmah are all named as descendants of Noah through his sons Shem, Ham, and Japheth. As I mentioned in the introduction, the goal of this book is not to present all the different interpretations of the events discussed in each chapter. The subject of this chapter would require its own chapter to cover all the various ways the names in Ezekiel 38–39 are interpreted. If you would like to further investigate the various interpretations of the Ezekiel war, I would suggest an excellent book on the subject by Dr. Mark Hitchcock, titled *Russia Rising*.[2]

My own research has led me to believe that the modern nations represented by these ancient names are as follows: Togarmah, Gomer, Meshech, and Tubal represent modern-day Turkey. Libya is, of course, modern Libya. Persia is Iran, and Ethiopia represents North Sudan (in Ezekiel's time Ethiopia was the area of North Africa directly south of Egypt). That leaves Magog and Rosh.

Flavius Josephus, the first-century Jewish historian, wrote, "Magog founded the Magogians, thus named after him, but who are by the Greeks called Scythians" (*Antiquities* 1.6.1). Because the Scythians' history is well documented, that has led some to see Magog as what is known as the southern steppes of Russia, which is today occupied by the nations of Kazakhstan, Kyrgyzstan, Uzbekistan, Turkmenistan, Tajikistan, and the northern parts of Afghanistan.

Going back to Genesis 10, we read this in verse 2: "The sons of Japheth were Gomer, Magog, Madai, Javan, Tubal, Meshech, and Tiras." There is little debate amongst scholars that Gomer, Tubal, and Meshech all settled in what is now modern-day Turkey. Madai is the ancestor of the Medes, who are the ancestors of the modern-day Kurds. The descendants of Javan settled in Greece. And it is unknown where Tiras, the grandson of Noah, and his people settled.

Magog is described by Strong's concordance as "the mountainous region between Cappadocia and Media." Cappadocia is in Turkey, and Media is in northwestern Iran. Thus, an argument could be made that Magog is the area between Cappadocia, Turkey, and Iranian Kurdistan and Azerbaijan (where Turkey, Iran, and Iraq share borders). Modern-day Armenia occupies a portion of this territory, as do eastern parts of Turkey. Though a popular interpretation for many years, I do not believe Magog represents modern-day Russia.

Here is what we know for sure: Whether Magog is eastern Turkey and Armenia or the former Soviet Republics at the southern steppes of Russia, both interpretations leave us with the single most important fact, and that is they are all predominantly Muslim nations.

What about Rosh and Gog? They are not found in the table of nations in Genesis 10. So who are they? For the answer, it's necessary for us to look at the opening of Ezekiel 38 using two different Bible versions:

> The word of the LORD came to me, saying, "Son of man, set your face against Gog, of the land of Magog, the prince of Rosh, Meshech, and Tubal, and prophesy against him, and say, 'Thus says the Lord GOD: "Behold, I am against you, O Gog, the prince of Rosh, Meshech, and Tubal.""'
>
> EZEKIEL 38:1-3 (NKJV)

> The word of the LORD came unto me, saying, Son of man, set thy face against Gog, the land of Magog, the chief prince of Meshech and Tubal, and prophesy against him, and say, Thus saith the Lord GOD; Behold, I am against thee, O Gog, the chief prince of Meshech and Tubal.
>
> EZEKIEL 38:1-3 (KJV)

First, we need to be careful about assuming that the mention of Gog in Revelation 20:8 means that the Ezekiel war is recorded there also. They are two distinct events, the battle theaters are different, the combatants are different, and the outcomes are different. Ezekiel 38–39 and Revelation 20 are not two records of the same battle.

With that said, why is Gog mentioned in both battle scenarios? One possibility is that Gog is a moniker for rulers who oppose Israel and lead battles against Jerusalem. Some say this could be a fallen angel who—as in Daniel 10:13, where the "prince of the kingdom of Persia" is identified as the one who hindered the delivery of the answer to Daniel's prayer—is assigned to harass the nation of Israel and incite hatred against the Jews and Jerusalem. Whichever case is true, it is clear that Gog is figurative of a leader who opposes God's people—whether that is God's chosen people the Jews (in the Ezekiel war scenario), or God's people the saints (who rule and reign in righteousness with Jesus during the millennium).

Rosh, as mentioned, is not named among the descendants of Noah in Genesis 10. The only time we find a person by that name is in Genesis 46:21, which lists the sons of Benjamin. The reason I quoted Ezekiel 38:1-3 in both the New King James Version and King James Version is because the word/name "Rosh" can be used in two different capacities. It can be a noun, meaning "head" or "chief," as the King James Bible translates it, And it can be a proper name, as in Genesis 46:21.

If rosh is indeed a noun and the King James Version rendering is right, that means that "Gog, [of] the land of Magog" who is the leader of Meshech and Tubal, will lead the invasion from the north into Israel.

> Persia, Ethiopia, and Libya are with them, all of them with shield and helmet; Gomer and all its troops; the house of Togarmah from the far north and all its troops—many people are with you.
>
> **EZEKIEL 38:5-6**

Meshech and Tubal are almost universally agreed upon as representing modern-day Turkey. The House of Togarmah relates to northeastern Turkey and Armenia. This means that the invasion is led by Turkey and not Russia, if rosh is indeed a noun and not a proper name. A key aspect of this is that if Russia is not involved, then the invading nations are all exclusively Muslim nations—Turkey, Iran, Sudan, and Libya.

If Rosh is not to be translated as a noun but as a proper name, that means Gog is the leader of Rosh, which most see as representing Russia. Again, Dr. Mark Hitchcock has done some excellent research on this. While there are 20 million Muslims in Russia, they account for only 13.5 percent of the total Russian population, which means Russia does not fit the predominantly Muslim profile of the other four nations.

Now, there are some nations that will protest the invasion of Israel:

> Sheba, Dedan, the merchants of Tarshish, and all their young lions will say to you, "Have you come to take plunder? Have you gathered your army to take booty, to carry away silver and gold, to take away livestock and goods, to take great plunder?"
>
> EZEKIEL 38:13

Sheba, Dedan, Tarshish, and their young lions represent Saudi Arabia and the Arab Gulf states. The one wild card among them is Tarshish, which could be Spain, at the far end of the Mediterranean Sea. Remember, Tarshish is where Jonah sought to flee to when God called him to preach to the ancient enemies of Israel, the Assyrians, in their capital city of Nineveh. Tarshish would be as far away as possible from Jonah's assigned mission field as he could go without leaving the Mediterranean.

Others see Tarshish as Great Britain, and thus among the "young lions" would be the United States. The main weakness with this view is the content of the protest: "Have you come to take plunder? Have you gathered...to take booty, to carry away silver and gold, to take away livestock and goods, to take great plunder?" The protesters ask,

"Is this invasion economically motivated?" With this in mind, to see Tarshish as Great Britain takes the protesting nations outside of the Mediterranean region and the oil- and natural gas-producing nations that round out the rest of the list. I personally do not see a place for Great Britain or the United States in the last-days prophetic scenario.

In light of all we see going on in the realm of energy-related products and the European market, this is where the Russia connection makes sense. Russia, Turkey, and Iran, the lead players in the invasion, all rely heavily on oil and natural gas products to fuel their economies, as do the nations that protest the invasion. This seems to be the common denominator of all the nations involved. Israel's entrance into these markets means competition, which, in turn, means price reductions. That would be the catalyst for the invading nations to attack Israel.

Those who interpret Russia as being Rosh make the argument that when you draw a line due north from Jerusalem on a world map, that line will run through Moscow. That is true. However, if you used a globe and ran a string or thread to the north pole from Jerusalem, the thread would run through Istanbul, Turkey—the former eastern capital of the Roman Empire. So which is it?

The argument for Russia is substantiated by this statement in Ezekiel 38:15: "You will come from your place out of the far north, you and many peoples with you, all of them riding on horses, a great company and a mighty army." With Rosh representing Russia, there is only one candidate among the nations named earlier that would qualify as being the most "far north" of them all—Russia.

The problem is this: "Gomer and all its troops; the house of Togarmah from the far north and all its troops—many people are with you" (Ezekiel 38:6). Ezekiel identifies who is in the far north as Togarmah, which, as we stated earlier, is in the region of modern-day Turkey. It seems a bit of a departure from the rules of Bible interpretation to say, in the same chapter and within the same context, that the far north can mean two different places. The other point we have to remember is that we cannot examine these prophecies through modern measures. Turkey would certainly qualify as being far north of Jerusalem in a pedestrian society. What's key is that the rules of biblical interpretation will not allow "from the far north" to mean Turkey in verse 6 and "out of the far north" to mean Russia in verse 15 of the same chapter and in the same context. But whether Russia is in or out changes nothing about how the scene plays out.

No matter who Gog represents, and regardless of whether Rosh is a proper name, noun, or adjective, the link between all the nations named in Ezekiel 38—the invading countries and the protesting countries—is the control of the flow of natural gas and crude-based products into Europe. This factor would determine the primary lens through which we should arrive at our interpretation of the events foretold in Ezekiel 38–39.

Some of the most frequently asked questions about the Ezekiel war are, When will it take place? Is it before the rapture? Is it before or during the tribulation? I do not know that we can answer those questions with absolute certainty, but it seems likely that because the three potential lead nations of the invasion, Russia, Turkey, and Iran, all have troops on the northern border of Israel, that the attack is not too far in the future. In addition, at the time of this writing, Russia has invaded Ukraine and taken control of the largest nuclear power plant in Europe. Consider also the fact that a number of nations are sanctioning Russia and refusing to buy their natural gas and petroleum products. This could be the "hooks" in the jaws (Ezekiel 38:4) that draws the invaders down from the north, and the last thing Russia wants from this invasion is a loss of market share. Israel is already making inroads into the Russian-dominated energy market by selling natural gas to Egypt, who in turn, is selling it to some of Russia's customer base.

Though we cannot be certain about when this war will start, it's clear that it will end during the tribulation. The reason this seems likely is evident in Ezekiel 38:

> "It will come to pass at the same time, when Gog comes against the land of Israel," says the Lord GOD, "that My fury will show in My face. For in My jealousy and in the fire of My wrath I have spoken: 'Surely in that day there shall be a great earthquake in the land of Israel, so that the fish of the sea, the birds of the heavens, the beasts of the field, all creeping things that creep on the earth, and all men who are on the face of the earth shall shake at My presence. The mountains shall be thrown down, the steep places shall fall, and every wall shall fall to the ground.' I will call for a sword against Gog throughout all My mountains," says the Lord GOD. "Every man's sword will be against his brother. And I will bring him to judgment with pestilence and bloodshed; I will rain down on him, on his troops, and on the many peoples who are with him, flooding rain, great hailstones, fire, and brimstone. Thus I will magnify Myself and sanctify Myself, and I will be known in the eyes of many nations. Then they shall know that I am the LORD."
>
> **EZEKIEL 38:18-23**

The response to the invasion of Israel is clearly divine in nature, and we do not find anything comparable to this during the church age. Keep in mind that there was no Israel to defend during the majority of the church age. And in this unprecedented season during which Israel and the church exist simultaneously, we saw Israel supernaturally protected and empowered by God when it was attacked by five Arab nations on the very night the Jewish nation declared statehood. We saw God protect Israel again in 1967 and 1973, when the Jewish people were far outgunned and outnumbered. And the people of Israel have experienced divine favor over the course of various battles against Lebanon and Gaza. However, there has never been direct divine intervention on the scale we read about in Ezekiel 38–39. The actions taken by God in response to the invasion of Israel are more consistent with the events of the tribulation (more in a moment).

Let's read Isaiah 17:1 and develop this further: "The burden against Damascus. 'Behold, Damascus will cease from being a city, and it will be a ruinous heap.'" There are some who argue that this prophecy was fulfilled when King Sennacherib's armies attacked Damascus in 689 BC. But this is easily refuted by the fact that Damascus still exists today—it is the capital of Syria. To cease from being a city means just that: it will no longer exist; it will not be rebuilt later under the same name in the same location. Today's inhabitants of Damascus claim bragging rights to being the oldest continuously inhabited city on earth, with a history of some 4,500 years. In other words, Isaiah 17:1 has not yet been fulfilled. Damascus has not yet become a "ruinous heap."

With that in mind, if we were to set a possible chronology based on the content of Ezekiel 38–39, it would likely unfold as follows: The destruction of Damascus would be the match that lights the Middle East powder keg. At the time of this writing, we know that Iran has troops in Syria. We also know that Israel has continually targeted weapons shipped from Iran to Syria for use against Israel. It is possible, and maybe even likely, that Israel's military will bring about the destruction of Damascus. This could be the event that Russia, Turkey, and Iran use as justification to invade Israel from their positions in Syria. And Libya and Sudan could attack from the south, or join the invading forces from either Lebanon or Syria.

There's one other point we should note. We're told in Ezekiel 38:6, "Gomer and all its troops; the house of Togarmah from the far north and all its troops—many people are with you." The word "people" in this verse can mean "nations" or "troops." This means that the invading forces might not be limited to the five nations mentioned earlier. This opens the door for a possible all-out Muslim invasion of Israel, or an attack by any energy-producing nation in the region that needs Israel's resources or to cut Israel off from the European market. Either way, it seems likely there will be some additional nations involved in the invasion.

There is no reason this attack could not happen before the rapture and outside the tribulation. It is possible that after this invasion, the rapture of the church will occur, and God will then shift His full attention toward Israel while the church is safe in heaven. It could be that then and only then God will respond in the manner we see described above. The one caveat we must consider is that the antichrist cannot rise to power until the hindering force of the Holy Spirit—through the church—is "taken out of the way" (2 Thessalonians 2:7).

One fact that is concrete is this: The church will not be present on earth for any of the antichrist's reign.

That does not mean that the antichrist will take over the world the day after the rapture. Rather, the tribulation will not begin until the antichrist makes a seven-year covenant with Israel, which he will break at the midpoint (Daniel 9:27). I believe the progression will likely be as follows: (1) the Ezekiel war begins, (2) the rapture of the church takes place, (3) the Ezekiel war is ended by God, and (4) the antichrist rises to power and says to the world, "Can't we all get along?" Then he will make a covenant or peace agreement with Israel, thus allowing the Jewish people to rebuild their temple. We'll talk more about what he does after this in our next chapter.

So again, it is possible, and maybe even probable, that the fulfillment of Isaiah 17:1 will lead to Ezekiel 38–39, which will then lead to Daniel 9:27 and Revelation 6:2. Admittedly, this is calculated speculation. But the one fact that is concrete is this: The church will not be present on earth for any of the antichrist's reign.

CHAPTER 7

THE MAN OF SIN

I n the previous chapter, we considered the possibility that the destruction of Damascus will be the fuse that ignites the Ezekiel war. We also noted that God's response to the nations that attack Israel will be very direct, setting it apart from the way He has interacted with Israel during this brief season that both Israel and the church have coexisted during the church age. We saw that it's possible the battle could begin before the end of the church age, and that it could conclude after the rapture of the church. This would allow for two developments to take place: the man of sin to rise to power, and the solution to the Middle East crisis to be offered in the form of a seven-year covenant. These two developments are described for us in the following passages:

> The mystery of lawlessness is already at work; only He who now restrains will do so until He is taken out of the way. And then the lawless one will be revealed, whom the Lord will consume with the breath of His mouth and destroy with the brightness of His coming. The coming of the lawless one is according to the working of Satan, with all power, signs, and lying wonders, and with all unrighteous

deception among those who perish, because they did not
receive the love of the truth, that they might be saved.

2 THESSALONIANS 2:7-10

He shall confirm a covenant with many for one week; but
in the middle of the week He shall bring an end to sacrifice
and offering. And on the wing of abominations shall be
one who makes desolate, even until the consummation,
which is determined, is poured out on the desolate.

DANIEL 9:27

Now I saw when the Lamb opened one of the seals; and
I heard one of the four living creatures saying with a
voice like thunder, "Come and see." And I looked, and
behold, a white horse. He who sat on it had a bow; and
a crown was given to him, and he went out conquering
and to conquer.

REVELATION 6:1-2

The covenant that finalizes the 70 weeks of Daniel will be presented to Israel and the world at the time Christ opens the first seal
of seven on the scroll described in Revelation chapter 5. There, the
apostle John tells us that he wept when, after a search of heaven
and earth among the living and the dead, no one was found worthy to open its seals. But then John said, "One of the elders said
to me, 'Do not weep. Behold, the Lion of the tribe of Judah, the
Root of David, has prevailed to open the scroll and to loose its
seven seals'" (verse 5).

The only one found worthy to loosen the seven seals on the scroll
is what John saw next: a Lamb standing as though it had been slain,
who is the Lion of the tribe of Judah (verses 5-6). When this worthy
one opens the first seal, the tribulation will begin. At that time, a rider

on a white horse will bring a pseudo-peace to the world by offering a seven-year covenant with Israel. This agreement will allow for the rebuilding of the Jewish temple on the Temple Mount, which has long been a point of contention between the Jews and the Muslim world.

In Revelation 6:2, the Greek word translated as "bow" is the same Greek word that is used in the Septuagint (the Greek translation of the Hebrew Old Testament) for "rainbow" in Genesis 9:12-15:

> God said: "This is the sign of the covenant which I make between Me and you, and every living creature that is with you, for perpetual generations: I set My rainbow in the cloud, and it shall be for the sign of the covenant between Me and the earth. It shall be, when I bring a cloud over the earth, that the rainbow shall be seen in the cloud; and I will remember My covenant which is between Me and you and every living creature of all flesh; the waters shall never again become a flood to destroy all flesh."

This gives us a biblical precedent of a "bow" or "rainbow" being a symbol of a covenant, and allows for us to understand that the bow in the hand of the rider on the white horse represents the seven-year covenant. It is this covenant that will usher in the seventieth and final week of the "seventy weeks...determined for [Daniel's] people and for [the] holy city," which is Jerusalem (Daniel 9:24). Before this can happen, the hindering force of the Holy Spirit—which is present on earth through the preserving and purifying influence of the church—must be removed. Then the Holy Spirit will no longer hold back the rise of the antichrist to power, and the church will no longer hold back the earth dwellers from the outbreak of utter lawlessness.

This is one of the major keys to establishing the pre-tribulation rapture position. The people of the church are temples of the Holy

Spirit, according to 1 Corinthians 6:19. And for the restraining force of the Holy Spirit to be "taken out of the way" (2 Thessalonians 2:7) so the antichrist can rise, the church cannot be present during any of the tribulation. This is why it is important for us to pair 2 Thessalonians 2:7-10 with Revelation 6:2. The rider on the white horse cannot present his covenant to Israel and the world while the church is still present on the earth.

There is one small interpretive insertion I would like to observe here before we move on. Some Bible readers believe there will be a break between the first and second riders of the four horsemen of the apocalypse, and have concluded that the pseudo-peace the antichrist brings will last for three-and-a-half years.

I do not agree with that for two reasons: First, nothing in the text indicates a break of 42 months in the advancement of the narrative between the riders of the first and second horses in Revelation 6. Second, in Revelation 13:5-6, we read this about the antichrist: "He was given a mouth speaking great things and blasphemies, and he was given authority to continue for forty-two months. Then he opened his mouth in blasphemy against God, to blaspheme His name, His tabernacle, and those who dwell in heaven."

Revelation 13:5 says the antichrist (the first beast) was given authority to continue for 42 months, and "then" he spoke blasphemies against God. If the 42 months here are "another" 42 months, or the second half of the tribulation, then the event described in verse 6 would happen *after* the 42 months had passed, which would put it at the end of the tribulation. The reason this timing is unlikely is that verse 6 describes the abomination of desolation, which marks the *midpoint* of the tribulation, according to Daniel 9:27, and will launch the second half of the tribulation.

While the book of Revelation, like the Genesis creation narrative, does not hold to a strict chronology, there is still an overall chronological order to it. The seventh seal on the scroll contains the seven trumpet judgments, and the seventh trumpet contains the seven bowl judgments, and so on. So if the beast is allowed to continue his actions for 42 months, *then* commit the abomination of desolation at the midpoint, there cannot be an extended time gap between the first and second horsemen of Revelation 6. That would mean nothing happens during the 42 months after Revelation 6:2. If that were so, the text would indicate that, but it doesn't. (We'll learn more about the four horsemen in the next chapter.)

So who is this first beast? What do we know about him? Let's address the *who* question first.

> I stood on the sand of the sea. And I saw a beast rising up out of the sea, having seven heads and ten horns, and on his horns ten crowns, and on his heads a blasphemous name. Now the beast which I saw was like a leopard, his feet were like the feet of a bear, and his mouth like the mouth of a lion. The dragon gave him his power, his throne, and great authority.
>
> **REVELATION 13:1-2**

While *antichrist* is the term we commonly ascribe to this figure, the Bible refers to this satanically empowered man as the first beast, with the second beast being the false prophet. The first beast will rise up out of the sea, an idiom that is often used in reference to the Gentile nations, but is also a frequent biblical reference to the Mediterranean. Some say the fact the first beast rises up from the sea means he is a Gentile, and others make the case that the antichrist, like his predecessor Antiochus Epiphanes, will be from Greece, which is bordered in part by the Mediterranean Sea. While both of these views are possible, the one fact we can know for sure about where this man comes from is found in the mention of the leopard, bear, and lion in the book of Daniel:

In the first year of Belshazzar king of Babylon, Daniel had a dream and visions of his head while on his bed. Then he wrote down the dream, telling the main facts.

Daniel spoke, saying, "I saw in my vision by night, and behold, the four winds of heaven were stirring up the Great Sea. And four great beasts came up from the sea, each different from the other. The first was like a lion, and had eagle's wings. I watched till its wings were plucked off; and it was lifted up from the earth and made to stand on two feet like a man, and a man's heart was given to it.

"And suddenly another beast, a second, like a bear. It was raised up on one side, and had three ribs in its mouth between its teeth. And they said thus to it: 'Arise, devour much flesh!'

"After this I looked, and there was another, like a leopard, which had on its back four wings of a bird. The beast also had four heads, and dominion was given to it.

"After this I saw in the night visions, and behold, a fourth beast, dreadful and terrible, exceedingly strong. It had huge iron teeth; it was devouring, breaking in pieces, and trampling the residue with its feet. It was different from all the beasts that were before it, and it had ten horns."

DANIEL 7:1-7

The lion, bear, and leopard are identified for us in Daniel 8. The lion represents the Babylonian Empire, the bear the Medo-Persian Empire, and the leopard the Greek Empire. The fourth beast, dreadful and terrible, is the Roman Empire that conquered all the geographic areas once held by the previous empires. The description in Revelation 13, which is recorded in reverse order because it is looking backward in time and not forward like Daniel, tells us the first beast will rise up from the former Roman Empire that will be revived during the tribulation.

We do not know the beast's nationality, though there are some who have speculated that he is Assyrian because of what is revealed by the prophet Micah:

> This One shall be peace.
>
> When the Assyrian comes into our land,
> and when he treads in our palaces,
> then we will raise against him
> seven shepherds and eight princely men.
> They shall waste with the sword the land of Assyria,
> and the land of Nimrod at its entrances;
> thus He shall deliver us from the Assyrian,
> when he comes into our land
> and when he treads within our borders.
>
> MICAH 5:5-6

In this passage, the mention of the Assyrian needs to be filtered through the lens of the fact that "Assyrian" was a term used to symbolize those who oppressed Israel. Nimrod and Assyria are synonyms in the passage above, and Ezra 6:22 refers to the king of Persia as the Assyrian. Artaxerxes, the third son of King Xerxes, was the Persian king who gave Nehemiah permission to repair the walls and gates of Jerusalem. His ethnicity was Persian, not Assyrian, and it was the Persian Empire that had defeated the Babylonians, and thus became Israel's oppressors. So Ezra called him the Assyrian, the oppressor.

Some argue that for the antichrist to be Assyrian also implies that he will be Muslim. There are two major problems with that. The first is that when Assyria was a world power, Islam did not exist yet. So a connection cannot be made between Assyrians and Islam. Second, the Jews would never consider making a covenant with a Muslim leader, and Islam, by definition, means "submission." Micah 5:5-6 is actually referring to the time when the "One [who] shall be peace" can *only* be the Prince of Peace, or Jesus, and to the peace He will bring during the millennium. Micah wasn't referring to the pseudo-peace at the beginning of the tribulation.

Perhaps one of the most challenging passages with regard to the identity of the antichrist is Revelation 13:18: "Here is wisdom. Let him who has understanding calculate the number of the beast, for it is the number of a man: His number is 666." The amount of ink and time that has been committed to "calculating" the number of the beast and thus exposing his identity is tremendous. In doing this, some Bible interpreters have employed what is known as gematria, a system of assigning numerical values to letters or words. In this way, they attempt to calculate the numerical value of a person's name or title and determine the identity of the antichrist. Caesar Nero has been suggested as a candidate, as has been Caligula. Some thought that former US president Ronald Wilson Reagan might be the antichrist because all three of his names have six letters each. And the list of speculative possibilities goes on and on.

The only definite fact we can know about the identity of the antichrist is that he will rise to power out of the revived Roman Empire. It is likely that neither he nor the second beast—the false prophet—will be Jews, because both of them will persecute the Jews. This raises a question: Why would the Jews be willing to work with a Gentile ruler who offers them a peace covenant? Think back to their appreciation for former President Donald Trump because he moved the US embassy to Jerusalem. Similarly, it is very possible that Israel would be willing to follow a Gentile leader who solves the Middle East crisis and allows for the third temple to be built.

While the identity of the first beast is mysterious, that's not the case about his actions, which are clearly described for us in Scripture. But before we examine some of them, we need to address an issue long debated amongst Bible scholars. This debate has to do with how we should understand Revelation 13:3: "I saw one of his heads as if it had been mortally wounded, and his deadly wound was healed. And all the world marveled and followed the beast."

There are three basic interpretations of this verse. First, this is a mock execution/resurrection scenario that attempts to mimic what happened to Jesus. Revelation 13:14 tells us the beast "was wounded by the sword and lived." Since Satan is a mimicker of God, this seems like a strong possibility, validated by what we just read. Second, some believe this means that a historical figure from the past (Caesar Nero is a popular candidate) will arise from the dead and rule the revived Roman Empire, which is beyond unlikely. The third interpretation is that the resurrected head that had a deadly wound that was healed speaks of the Roman Empire itself, which is also possible.

Revelation 13:1 says the beast will have "seven heads and ten horns." The seven heads refer to empires from the past that oppressed Israel, beginning with Egypt, followed by Assyria, then Babylon, Medo-Persia, Greece, and Rome. That is six empires, with the former Roman Empire being included, and the once-dead Roman Empire springing back to life during the tribulation rounds out the seven. The horns with ten crowns in Revelation 13:1 point to Revelation 17:8-14:

> The beast that you saw was, and is not, and will ascend out of the bottomless pit and go to perdition. And those who dwell on the earth will marvel, whose names are not written in the Book of Life from the foundation of the world, when they see the beast that was, and is not, and yet is.
>
> Here is the mind which has wisdom: The seven heads are seven mountains on which the woman sits. There are also

seven kings. Five have fallen, one is, and the other has not yet come. And when he comes, he must continue a short time. The beast that was, and is not, is himself also the eighth, and is of the seven, and is going to perdition.

The ten horns which you saw are ten kings who have received no kingdom as yet, but they receive authority for one hour as kings with the beast. These are of one mind, and they will give their power and authority to the beast. These will make war with the Lamb, and the Lamb will overcome them, for He is Lord of lords and King of kings; and those who are with Him are called, chosen, and faithful.

Again, we see the oppressive empires of Israel's past, of which five had fallen and one is. The five are Egypt, Assyria, Babylon, Medo-Persia, and Greece. The "one is" refers to the Roman Empire, which dominated the world at the time John wrote Revelation. And there is one that "has not yet come." Verse 11 says, "The beast that was, and is not, is himself also the eighth, and is of the seven." That is, the eighth refers to the beast himself, who is the head of the seventh kingdom, the revived Roman Empire.

As mentioned earlier, at the time of this writing, Russia has invaded Ukraine, and for the first time in its history, the European Union is no longer operating like a dysfunctional family, but is unified in its stand against Russia. This could lead to a permanent change in the union's level of cooperation, bringing the different nations closer together as a single unit.

We need to do a bit more interpretive housekeeping here based on the fact that currently, there are 27 members in the European Union (EU). For help, let's turn to Daniel chapter 2:

Whereas you saw the feet and toes, partly of potter's clay and partly of iron, the kingdom shall be divided; yet the strength of the iron shall be in it, just as you saw the iron mixed with ceramic clay. And as the toes of the feet were partly of iron and partly of clay, so the kingdom shall be partly strong and partly fragile. As you saw iron mixed with ceramic clay, they will mingle with the seed of men; but they will not adhere to one another, just as iron does not mix with clay. And in the days of these kings the God of heaven will set up a kingdom which shall never be destroyed; and the kingdom shall not be left to other people; it shall break in pieces and consume all these kingdoms, and it shall stand forever.

DANIEL 2:41-44

The statue in Daniel 2 has feet and toes, and because the statue is of a person, we can conclude it has ten toes. With that in mind, some people have been waiting for the EU to be reduced to ten nations. It is from this ten-nation federation partly of iron (the former Roman Empire) and of clay (other nations) that the antichrist will arise. If the ten toes are a mixture of iron and clay, that frees the interpretation from being limited to ten in number. That means we don't have to wait for some kind of shakeup in the EU that reduces the number of nations to ten so that the prophetic narrative can advance.

One other point to remember is this: Revelation 17:12 tells us, "The ten horns which you saw are ten kings who have received no kingdom as yet, but they receive authority for one hour as kings with the beast." The ten kings who rule for "one hour"—meaning a short time—with the antichrist will help rule a geopolitical landscape restructured by the antichrist. They will have received no kingdom as of yet, and their assignments will come from the first beast himself. There will likely be no China, Russia, United States, Canada, etc., for the beast will divide the world into ten kingdoms centered on his rule based in the geographic region of the former Roman

Empire. This also tells us we should not waste time trying to figure out who the antichrist's ten cronies might be. As Revelation 17:12 says, they are not current world leaders. They have not received a kingdom as of yet.

Revelation 13:16-18 tells us more about the antichrist's rule:

> He causes all, both small and great, rich and poor, free and slave, to receive a mark on their right hand or on their foreheads, and that no one may buy or sell except one who has the mark or the name of the beast, or the number of his name.
>
> Here is wisdom. Let him who has understanding calculate the number of the beast, for it is the number of a man: His number is 666.

The beast will control global commerce through the institution of a system that identifies those who have sided with him and his rule via a mark on the right hand or forehead. The Greek word translated "mark" means "a brand or etching." It could be an interactive implant, a biometric tattoo, or simply an identifying mark on a person's hand or forehead. The fact that our world has been increasingly indoctrinated toward accepting greater levels of governmental control—via mandates like those that were imposed during the COVID pandemic—should help us to realize that the exercise of global control over all people is now possible. The technological elements necessary for such control have long been in place. A major example of this are the "point of sale" devices that are now everywhere, including handheld mobile devices.

The extent of the antichrist's power is also evident in Revelation 13:15, which tells us that anyone who does "not worship the image of the beast [will] be killed." In light of what has happened in world history, it's not too hard to imagine one person putting millions of others to death. Our world has seen its fair share of brutal dictators. But what's chilling here is that the antichrist's insistence upon killing everyone who refuses to worship him will be supported by all the "earth dwellers" who are loyal to him. They will be on board with his kind of thinking.

We have been watching our world move more and more in this direction. As governments impose mandates, people are in favor of punishing those who don't comply. That happened during the COVID pandemic. There were many who not only supported the restrictions imposed on the unvaccinated, but also called for the punishment of them.

Not only will the man of sin demand political loyalty, but worship as well, of which God alone is worthy. Usually we think of the term *worship* in connection with music, but the word itself means "to prostrate one's self and submit." The beast will demand total reverence and compliance from his subjects, and those who refuse to worship him will pay with their lives.

> I saw thrones, and they sat on them, and judgment was committed to them. Then I saw the souls of those who had been beheaded for their witness to Jesus and for the word of God, who had not worshiped the beast or his image, and had not received his mark on their foreheads or on their hands. And they lived and reigned with Christ for a thousand years.
>
> **REVELATION 20:4**

This should remind us that Satan comes only to steal, kill, and destroy, and the fact that the man of sin will be satanically empowered indicates he will do as his master does. Those who refuse to worship him will be beheaded. The Greek text here does not refer to the clean, quick kind of beheading done with a guillotine or a large Arabian-type saber. The word means "to chop off with an axe," which implies brutality within the act of beheading. The tribulation will be a time of unparalleled brutality, which we'll examine more closely in the next chapter.

Satan comes only to steal, kill, and destroy, and the fact that the man of sin will be satanically empowered indicates he will do as his master does.

Someday, the church is going to be removed from earth, and a man is going to ride onto the world scene offering a covenant that will bring a temporary peace. He will demand that he be worshipped, and refusal will mean death. His constituents will be on board with this kind of punishment, as will those he selects to rule with him during his short reign of terror.

The whole world will be deluded into worshipping the antichrist because of his supposedly deadly wound that will be healed. The same people who express loyalty to him will have consciously rejected the one who died for their sins, rose from the dead, and ascended into heaven that they might live forever. The world is ready for the man of sin; it's evident in the mentality and spiritual condition of the earth dwellers around us. They are more than ready to be deceived by someone who performs false signs and wonders that fascinate them all. And the technological capabilities are in place as well.

If the world is ready for the antichrist, that means the church needs to be ready to meet Jesus Christ in the air, where we will join the dead in Christ, who will rise first. Then we will all be with the Lord forever.

What happens after the rider on the white horse rides onto the world scene? Buckle up, because things are going to go downhill fast from this point forward!

CHAPTER 8

THE SEVENTIETH SEVEN

I am sure the debate over the timing of the rapture will rage until it happens—and at that point, everyone will be pre-trib (wink wink). But one of the most significant supports for belief in the pre-tribulation rapture view is one of the most seldom offered. Let's look at it now.

> Seventy weeks are determined for your people and for your holy city, to finish the transgression, to make an end of sins, to make reconciliation for iniquity, to bring in everlasting righteousness, to seal up vision and prophecy, and to anoint the Most Holy.
>
> Know therefore and understand, that from the going forth of the command to restore and build Jerusalem until Messiah the Prince, there shall be seven weeks and sixty-two weeks; the street shall be built again, and the wall, even in troublesome times.
>
> And after the sixty-two weeks Messiah shall be cut off, but not for Himself; and the people of the prince who is to come shall destroy the city and the sanctuary. The end of it

shall be with a flood, and till the end of the war desolations
are determined. Then he shall confirm a covenant with
many for one week; but in the middle of the week he shall
bring an end to sacrifice and offering. And on the wing
of abominations shall be one who makes desolate, even
until the consummation, which is determined, is poured
out on the desolate.

DANIEL 9:24-27

In this passage, the Hebrew word translated "weeks" literally means
"a heptad," which is a set or group of seven. It could refer to seven
hours, days, weeks, months, or years; it could mean seven objects.
The context here reveals the meaning to be a seven-year period, based
on the calendar date mentioned when the command to rebuild the
wall around Jerusalem was given. We also need to note that the word
"determined" means "to decree" or "to mark out." Daniel was told by
the angel Gabriel that 70 seven-year periods were decreed, or marked
out, for Daniel's people, the Jews, and Daniel's holy city, Jerusalem.

This declaration is followed by a breakdown of how the weeks will
unfold: first, there will be seven periods of seven years. Then there
will be 62 periods of seven years. Then we come to a passage about
the death of the Messiah and, later on, the destruction of Jerusalem,
which took place in AD 70. Jerusalem was destroyed by "the people of the prince who is to come" (the beast of Revelation 13, as we
saw in the previous chapter). This man of sin will rise up from the
revived Roman Empire, which will be occupied by descendants of
the people who were in power at the time of the Messiah's crucifixion. The antichrist will establish a covenant with Israel for a period
of seven years, which will usher in the seventieth seven, or the final
week of Daniel's 70 weeks.

The point about the pre-tribulation rapture "proof" in this passage is this: The church was not present on earth during the first 69

seven-year periods, so why would it be present for the seventieth? This final week is marked out by God for Daniel's people and the holy city of Jerusalem. The seventieth seven is the tribulation, also called the time of Jacob's trouble (*not* Jacob's and the church's trouble). During this time, God will discipline the nation of Israel and pour out His judgment on a Christ-rejecting world. It will be a period unlike any other in the history of mankind.

Matthew 24:22 tells us that "unless those days were shortened, no flesh would be saved; but for the elect's sake those days will be shortened." The elect, in this context, refers to believing Jews who, at Christ's return, will recognize that Jesus of Nazareth, the one whom they pierced (Zechariah 12:10), is in fact the Holy One of Israel, their Savior.

Daniel 9 also mentions that at the mid-point of the seventieth seven, the antichrist will break the covenant made with Israel and commit what Jesus referred to as the "abomination of desolation."

> When you see the "abomination of desolation," spoken of by Daniel the prophet, standing in the holy place (whoever reads, let him understand), then let those who are in Judea flee to the mountains. Let him who is on the housetop not go down to take anything out of his house. And let him who is in the field not go back to get his clothes. But woe to those who are pregnant and to those who are nursing babies in those days! And pray that your flight may not be in winter or on the Sabbath. For then there will be great tribulation, such as has not been since the beginning of the world until this time, no, nor ever shall be.
>
> **MATTHEW 24:15-21**

The man of sin, the first beast of Revelation 13, will make a covenant with Israel that allows the Jewish people to rebuild their temple.

Then at the midpoint of this covenant, he will enter the Most Holy Place, where the Ark of the Covenant was housed, and declare that he himself is God. Jesus warns the Jews that when that happens, they are to run, "for then there will be great tribulation," such as has never been since the world began.

It is because of this passage that some people see the first 42 months or 1,260 days of the tribulation as a time during which the world will enjoy a pseudo-peace brought about by the covenant that settles the Middle East crisis. While there are clearly two halves to the seventieth seven, we should not press the meaning of Matthew 24:15-21 too far and conclude that only the second part of the seventieth seven will see God's wrath. As we learned earlier, the seal judgments will begin right at the start of the tribulation, in Revelation 6, and God's wrath will be expressed all through the seven-year period. But we also know that the second half of the seventieth seven will be a time of unprecedented cataclysmic events on the earth, and we have to remember that God's wrath has multiple forms.

> The wrath of God is revealed from heaven against all ungodliness and unrighteousness of men, who suppress the truth in unrighteousness, because what may be known of God is manifest in them, for God has shown it to them. For since the creation of the world His invisible attributes are clearly seen, being understood by the things that are made, even His eternal power and Godhead, so that they are without excuse, because, although they knew God, they did not glorify Him as God, nor were thankful, but became futile in their thoughts, and their foolish hearts were darkened. Professing to be wise, they became fools.
>
> **ROMANS 1:18-22**

Therefore God also gave them up to uncleanness, in the lusts of their hearts, to dishonor their bodies among themselves.

ROMANS 1:24

For this reason God gave them up to vile passions. For even their women exchanged the natural use for what is against nature.

ROMANS 1:26

Even as they did not like to retain God in their knowledge, God gave them over to a debased mind, to do those things which are not fitting.

ROMANS 1:28

In Romans chapter 1, the wrath of God manifested itself in the form of giving God-deniers up to uncleanness and vile passions, and then turning them over to a debased mind and all the behaviors that come with that. I point this out so we can understand that God's wrath is not manifested solely through global cataclysmic events. For instance, the first act of God's wrath during the seventieth seven will be this:

I saw when the Lamb opened one of the seals; and I heard one of the four living creatures saying with a voice like thunder, "Come and see." And I looked, and behold, a white horse. He who sat on it had a bow; and a crown was given to him, and he went out conquering and to conquer.

REVELATION 6:1-2

As soon as the first seal is opened, the man of sin will ride onto the world scene with a covenant in hand. This horseman's arrival will be part of God's consequential wrath, which is consistent with the message of Romans 1: Reject God, and there will be consequences. The seventieth seven may not be filled from beginning to end with asteroids and earthquakes or comets and a scorching sun, but everything that occurs will be part of God's wrath. We could even think about it this way: God's removal of the church from earth will be an act of His consequential wrath because the church is the world's only source of salt and light. The rapture will leave the world without the preserving and purifying influence of the church.

God's removal of the church from earth will be an act of His consequential wrath because the church is the world's only source of salt and light.

With that understood, what will the cataclysmic wrath of God look like during the seventieth seven? After the covenant-bearing rider on the white horse arrives and brings a pseudo-peace to the world, it won't be long before that comes to a quick end.

> When He opened the second seal, I heard the second living creature saying, "Come and see." Another horse, fiery red, went out. And it was granted to the one who sat on it to take peace from the earth, and that people should kill one another; and there was given to him a great sword.
>
> When He opened the third seal, I heard the third living creature say, "Come and see." So I looked, and behold, a black horse, and he who sat on it had a pair of scales in his hand. And I heard a voice in the midst of the four living creatures saying, "A quart of wheat for a denarius,

and three quarts of barley for a denarius; and do not harm the oil and the wine."

When He opened the fourth seal, I heard the voice of the fourth living creature saying, "Come and see." So I looked, and behold, a pale horse. And the name of him who sat on it was Death, and Hades followed with him. And power was given to them over a fourth of the earth, to kill with sword, with hunger, with death, and by the beasts of the earth.

REVELATION 6:3-8

Remember: All that takes place between Revelation 6:1 and Revelation 19:11 (when Jesus returns with the church) will occur within seven sets of 360 days, or Jewish calendar years. And they will happen in immediate or near-immediate succession. That means that within the opening moments of the seventieth seven, one-quarter of the earth's population will die.

The rider on the fiery red horse will take peace from the earth. This is why those who think the rider on the white horse is Jesus are in error. When Jesus brings peace, it will last forever—no one will take it away. We also need to note that during the red horseman's ride, people will kill one another. This does not refer to international conflict; rather, it's exactly what the text says: people will "kill one another." The Greek word translated "kill" means "to butcher." It is the word used to describe an animal being killed for a sacrifice. When the rider on the red horse is unleashed, all moral boundaries will be cast off, and people will butcher each other like animals.

As Matthew 24:12 says, "Lawlessness will abound, [and] the love of many will grow cold." Remember, those who love the Lord will be taken up in the rapture. This will leave the world filled with God-hating earth dwellers who are without the natural familial love that once existed while Christians were still on earth. I cannot think of a better proof that we are close to such a time of widespread murder than the fact that many people promote and protect the right to kill an unborn child in the womb of its mother. This tells us, as do many other things, that natural affection is waning in mankind.

Next, the rider on the black horse will bring a famine that goes on to cause devastating inflation all over the world. These seasons of murder and famine will be followed by the rider on the pale horse. The Greek word for "pale" is *chloros* and means "sickly green." It's the word used to describe the color of a decomposing body. Exacerbated by the previous events, diseases will spread worldwide, and the scarcity of food will cause the animal kingdom and humans to compete for the dwindling food supply, killing off one-fourth of the earth's population.

These are just three of the 21 judgments that will come upon the earth during the tribulation, and a bit later in the same chapter of Revelation, we read about how people will react:

> The kings of the earth, the great men, the rich men, the
> commanders, the mighty men, every slave and every free
> man, hid themselves in the caves and in the rocks of the
> mountains, and said to the mountains and rocks, "Fall
> on us and hide us from the face of Him who sits on the
> throne and from the wrath of the Lamb! For the great day
> of His wrath has come, and who is able to stand?"
>
> REVELATION 6:15-17

After the four horsemen of the apocalypse comes the cry of the tribulation martyrs, who ask God, "'How long, O Lord, holy and true, until You judge and avenge our blood on those who dwell on the earth?' Then a white robe was given to each of them; and it was said to them that they should rest a little while longer," for their number was going to increase (Revelation 6:10-11). Next comes a massive earthquake, followed by a meteor shower that drives people to hide in the caves and rocks of the mountains and cry out for the rocks and mountains to hide them from the wrath of God and the Lamb. They do not call out to God for mercy; they do not repent of their evil deeds. Instead, they cry out to the earth to protect them.

The reason this is important is because it reveals the heart condition of those who enter the tribulation, which has barely begun. Their hearts are so hard they would rather pray to nature than to the God who created everything. We live in a time when even religious leaders of the world are calling for climate care and the love of "Mother Earth." There is talk of implementing climate-change lockdown in cities—people will be given a certain number of miles they are allowed to travel per year, and they will not be allowed to leave the city if they exceed those miles. This tells us of the grave spiritual condition of humanity by the time the seventieth seven arrives. Much of mankind will be worshipping the earth rather than the one who made it.

As the world is being prepared morally and spiritually for the seventieth seven, it is also moving progressively toward the cataclysmic events that will occur during that time. Here's what Jesus said when four of His disciples asked Him about this:

> Now as He sat on the Mount of Olives, the disciples came to Him privately, saying, "Tell us, when will these things be? And what will be the sign of Your coming, and of the end of the age?" And Jesus answered and said to them: "Take heed that no one deceives you. For many will come in My name, saying, 'I am the Christ,' and will deceive many. And you will hear of wars and rumors of wars. See that you are not troubled; for all these things must come to pass, but the end is not yet. For nation will rise against nation, and kingdom against kingdom. And there will be

famines, pestilences, and earthquakes in various places. All these are the beginning of sorrows."

MATTHEW 24:3-8

As we consider what is to come, we're reminded that there are some who argue that such problems have always been with us. They say, "There have always been wars, international and ethnic strife, famine, diseases, and earthquakes." That is true; however, we need to remember that the questions asked by the four disciples had to do with the last days and the signs of Jesus' coming, not the general history of the world. Note that Jesus said these events would be "the beginning of sorrows," which could also be translated "the commencement of labor pains." This indicates His answer was specific to the disciples' questions—it was about the signs of His coming and the end of the age.

This tells us that these normal, course-of-life events will take on special significance in relation to the signs pertaining to last days. And Jesus' remark about labor pains tells us these events will increase in frequency and intensity. While we could cite statistics that confirm increases in earthquakes, diseases, famines, and wars, we need to recognize that the ultimate of these events will occur during the seventieth seven. The greatest war ever in human history will happen at the end of the tribulation, the greatest earthquake will happen during that period, as will the greatest famine, and so on.

There is another element of the tribulation that the world is being indoctrinated for, which we will discuss in a moment. But first, here is a rundown of what will happen after the events described in Revelation 6:

- Revelation 7 tells us there will be a pause in the catastrophic judgments. Angels will hold back the "four winds of the earth" (verse 1), and no more harm will occur to the earth until the 12,000 virgin men from each of the 12 tribes of Israel are sealed.

- In Revelation 8, the seventh seal is opened, and seven angels who stand before God with seven trumpets are revealed.

- When the first trumpet sounds, hail and fire mingled with blood will strike the earth, and one-third of the trees and all the green grass on the earth will be burned up.

- At the sounding of the second trumpet, an asteroid will fall into the sea, one-third of the sea will become blood, one-third of the living creatures in the sea will die, and one-third of the world's ships will be destroyed.

- At the blast of the third trumpet, a comet will strike the earth and poison one-third of the world's fresh water supply, likely with radiation.

- When the fourth angel blows his trumpet, one-third of the sun, moon, and stars will be darkened. And an angel will fly through the midst of heaven, saying with a loud voice, "Woe, woe, woe to the inhabitants of the earth, because of the remaining blasts of the trumpet." In other words, God's judgments will progressively get more intense, like labor pains.

- The fifth trumpet will unleash a swarm of locusts from the bottomless pit to torment humanity for five months but not kill anyone. The locusts will do no harm to the earth itself, but their sting will be so painful that people seek death but cannot find it.

- The sixth angel's trumpet blast will release four angels who "are bound at the great river Euphrates" (Revelation 9:14) to release an army of 200 million horsemen, who will kill one-third of mankind.

Even after all this takes place, notice how those who manage to survive will respond:

> The rest of mankind, who were not killed by these plagues, did not repent of the works of their hands, that they should not worship demons, and idols of gold, silver, brass, stone, and wood, which can neither see nor hear nor walk. And they did not repent of their murders or their sorceries or their sexual immorality or their thefts.
>
> REVELATION 9:20-21

Next, we read of another mighty angel coming down from heaven, and seven thunders will sound (Revelation 10:1-4). Then the angel standing on the sea and the land will raise his hand to heaven and swear by the one who lives forever and ever that, in the days of the sounding of the seventh trumpet, the mystery of God will be finished that He spoke of through His prophets. This means the seventh trumpet will release the fullness of God's undiluted wrath on the earth.

Let's pause here. Consider that so far, almost two-thirds of the world's population has been killed by the cataclysmic wrath of God. There are those who say that the "last trumpet" of 1 Corinthians 15:52 is the seventh trumpet of Revelation, and they say this is when the rapture will happen.

> Behold, I tell you a mystery: We shall not all sleep, but we shall all be changed— in a moment, in the twinkling of an eye, at the last trumpet. For the trumpet will sound, and the dead will be raised incorruptible, and we shall be changed.
>
> 1 CORINTHIANS 15:51-52

But this view is hard to reconcile with the fact that 1 Thessalonians 5:9 says the church is not appointed to God's wrath. The last trumpet of 1 Corinthians 15:52 is the trumpet that will signal the end of the time of the Gentiles and the church age. It will not sound during the tribulation, for the man of sin, whose rise to power begins the tribulation, cannot come on the scene until the church is removed. Remember as well that the seventieth seven is determined for Daniel's people and the holy city (Daniel 9:24). The church was not present on the earth during the first 69 sevens, and won't be on the earth during any of the seventieth seven either.

Resuming our rundown, here's what will take place:

- Revelation 11 tells of the ministry, death, and resurrection of God's two witnesses. Then the seventh angel will sound his trumpet, and loud voices in heaven will proclaim, "The kingdoms of this world have become the kingdoms of our Lord and of His Christ, and He shall reign forever and ever!" (verse 15).

- Revelation 12 describes God's supernatural protection of Israel and Satan's getting thrown out of heaven and down to the earth, and his angels with him.

- Revelation 13 reports the rise of the first and second beasts to power.

- Revelation 14 gives more details about the 144,000 protected Jewish witnesses. Then we read of how the earth will be harvested in preparation for the full and final judgments of God in the form of seven bowls of wrath (which are described in Revelation 16):

  » The first bowl will cause loathsome sores on the bodies of those who took the mark of the beast.

» The second bowl will turn the sea into blood and kill every living creature in the sea.

» The third bowl will turn all the fresh waters of the earth into blood.

» The fourth bowl will lead the sun to scorch the inhabitants of the earth (most likely a coronal mass ejection that will cause radiation burns on people's skin).

» The fifth bowl will bring darkness and cold. This will cause the burned skin of mankind to be so painful that people gnaw their tongues in agony and blaspheme God.

» The sixth bowl will dry up the Euphrates River, making way for the kings from the east to gather for the battle "of that great day of God Almighty" (Revelation 16:14).

» The seventh bowl will unleash the greatest earthquake ever to strike the earth.

All of this will be followed by the fall of Babylon and the second coming of Christ.

We have all heard the saying, "You don't know what you're missing." If you know Jesus as your Lord and Savior, you do know. The rapture will spare us from God's wrath.

The reason for compacting all of God's judgments in the manner that I've just listed them is to communicate how they will occur in quick succession, all within the time period of the seventieth seven. Reading through them this way should help us to realize what a devastating time the tribulation will be. This should create in us a sense of urgency for telling others they need to get right with God through Jesus Christ before that time comes.

The good news is that the church will not be here for any portion of the tribulation for multiple reasons—not the least of which is this: "Because you have kept My command to persevere, I also will keep you from the hour of trial which shall come upon the whole world, to test those who dwell on the earth" (Revelation 3:10).

We could spend hundreds of hours and use thousands of words to describe the details of the events prophesied in Revelation. The majority of what will happen is exclusive to the seventieth seven. And there are no signs that indicate these specific events are drawing near, such as the locust hoard from the bottomless pit, or the darkness and painful cold that will strike the earth. But there is one item in particular that we do need to highlight that the world is being prepared for even now. (If you are born again, you've no need to prepare—just be aware.)

> He causes all, both small and great, rich and poor, free and slave, to receive a mark on their right hand or on their foreheads, and that no one may buy or sell except one who has the mark or the name of the beast, or the number of his name. Here is wisdom. Let him who has understanding calculate the number of the beast, for it is the number of a man: His number is 666.
>
> **REVELATION 13:16-18**

We have been watching a global shift take place that is unprecedented due to the COVID pandemic. The scare caused by the spread of the virus caused a divided world to become more united in the search for solutions. The information age in which we live allowed for a new level of communication to take place that was not possible with previous generations that experienced pandemics. International travel was restricted, and buying and selling was limited in many places to those who had a "proof of vaccination" card. Neither the vaccine nor the card are the mark of the beast, but they normalized the idea that a global governmental body could determine who can buy and sell.

Also advanced during the pandemic was the thinking that those who expressed skepticism about the vaccines or did not get vaccinated were enemies and were causing the pandemic to spread. But in time, it was confirmed that the vaccinated were spreading COVID too. Some people called for the imprisonment of the unvaccinated, and others said they should be denied medical care if they got sick—which, in essence, means they deserved to die.

During the tribulation, those who refuse the mark of the beast will be put to death by beheading, and earth dwellers will agree this is a deserved punishment. The seventieth seven will be a time of unprecedented human evil against the Jews and those who follow Jesus. There are already many people who think that if someone doesn't "go along with the system," they deserve to die. Antisemitism is also on the rise, and some have even blamed the pandemic on the Jews.

> There are already many people who think
> that if someone doesn't "go along with
> the system," they deserve to die.

While it's hard to read about such things, there is one important point we need to remember about the wrath of Almighty God—a point made evident in Exodus:

> In that day I will set apart the land of Goshen, in which
> My people dwell, that no swarms of flies shall be there,
> in order that you may know that I am the LORD in the
> midst of the land.
>
> EXODUS 8:22

> "I will harden Pharaoh's heart, so that he will pursue them;
> and I will gain honor over Pharaoh and over all his army,
> that the Egyptians may know that I am the LORD." And
> they did so.
>
> EXODUS 14:4

The plagues of Egypt had a twofold purpose: to show Pharaoh and the Egyptians that the God of Israel is the true and living God, and to show the Israelites that their God is the Lord. He did this by "setting apart" the land of Goshen, where the enslaved Israelites lived during the Egyptian captivity. In this way, God supernaturally and sovereignly protected His people from the wrath poured out on the Egyptians. This was to serve as evidence that He was the Lord.

This will be the end result of the seventieth seven as well. God will protect the remnant of Jews who will believe during the tribulation. Zechariah 13:8 says two-thirds of the Jews will die during that time, but they will die in unbelief. In verse 9, God says, "I will bring the one-third through the fire, will refine them as silver is refined, and test them as gold is tested. They will call on My name, and I will answer them. I will say, 'This is My people'; and each one will say, 'The LORD is my God.'"

The one-third of the Jews who survive the seventieth seven will come to the conclusion that the Lord is their God and that Jesus Christ is the Lord. What will bring them to this place? God's protection during His time of wrath. Zechariah 12:10 tells us what will happen: "I will pour on the house of David and on the inhabitants of Jerusalem the Spirit of grace and supplication; then they will look on Me whom they pierced. Yes, they will mourn for Him as one mourns for his only son, and grieve for Him as one grieves for a firstborn."

The apostle Paul said in Romans 11:26 that "all Israel will be saved," and Zechariah 12:10 recorded how and when this will occur, which is at the second coming of Jesus. Yet tragically, there is an errant teaching coming out of the church today known as dual covenant theology. This theology teaches that Jews may simply keep the law of Moses and don't need Christ because of the "everlasting covenant" (Genesis 17:13) between Abraham and God, whereas Gentiles must convert to Christianity.

The problems with this thinking are worthy of an entire book, but let me say this as briefly as possible: This is nothing short of anti-semitism in the most heinous manner. It communicates a lie to the Jews—from the church—that they can be saved apart from being born again. Remember what Jesus told Nicodemus, the teacher of Israel, in John 3:3? "Most assuredly, I say to you, unless one is born again, he cannot see the kingdom of God."

Keep in mind that the law had no provision in it to save the human soul. Paul said in Romans 3:20, "By the deeds of the law no flesh will be justified in His sight, for by the law is the knowledge of sin." Keeping the law doesn't save you; it shows you need a Savior. And the world's only Savior is Christ the Lord.

Dual covenant theology has another problem: If all Israel will be saved through the law, and less than 5 percent of Jews are Orthodox and attempt to keep the law, how are the other 95 percent of the Jews going to be saved? What about ethnic Jews like my dear friend and brother Amir Tsarfati, who is a born-again Christian and does not keep the law? How will he be saved? What about Peter, James, and John, and the other apostles—all Jews who were born again and were not under the law?

At the second coming of Jesus Christ to the earth, when His feet touch down on the Mount of Olives, the mountain will split in two, and living waters will flow from it, bringing life back to the seas and earth. And the one-third of the Jews who were supernaturally protected by God because they would come to believe in Jesus as Messiah will look upon Him whom their ancestors pierced, and they will mourn as one would the loss of an only child. When this happens, all Israel will be saved!

There are myriad other things that will happen at the return of Christ, and we will discuss them in detail in the next chapter.

CHAPTER 9

THE SECOND COMING

I can say with confidence that, after more than 35 years of teaching the Bible and countless sermons, the most frequently quoted verses that have found their way into sermons are these:

> Now I saw heaven opened, and behold, a white horse. And He who sat on him was called Faithful and True, and in righteousness He judges and makes war. His eyes were like a flame of fire, and on His head were many crowns. He had a name written that no one knew except Himself. He was clothed with a robe dipped in blood, and His name is called The Word of God. And the armies in heaven, clothed in fine linen, white and clean, followed Him on white horses. Now out of His mouth goes a sharp sword, that with it He should strike the nations. And He Himself will rule them with a rod of iron. He Himself treads the winepress of the fierceness and wrath of Almighty God. And He has on His robe and on His thigh a name written:
>
> KING OF KINGS AND LORD OF LORDS.
>
> **REVELATION 19:11-16**

There is much we can glean from these magnificent verses, and the first is that this rider on a white horse is not the same rider seen in Revelation 6:2. That rider is the antichrist; this rider is Jesus Christ. We know this for many reasons, but the most obvious is this rider is identified as the Word of God—a moniker attributed to Jesus in John 1:1. The fact that He wears many crowns establishes His supreme and absolute authority. He is the faithful and true one, He judges and makes war, He will strike the nations with the sword of His Word, and He alone treads the winepress of the fierce wrath of Almighty God. This pretty much does away with any idea that Jesus is more passive than the angry, wrathful God of the Old Testament. Jesus and the Father are one, including in their judicial and retributive nature. John 5:22 tells us this about Jesus as judge: "The Father judges no one, but has committed all judgment to the Son."

Jesus first came as the Lamb of God to take away the sins of the world (John 1:29). But He is coming back as the Lion of Judah to judge the world and make war with His enemies. We are coming back with Him and are identified as the "armies in heaven, clothed in fine linen, white and clean" (Revelation 19:14).

> I heard, as it were, the voice of a great multitude, as the sound of many waters and as the sound of mighty thunderings, saying, "Alleluia! For the Lord God Omnipotent reigns! Let us be glad and rejoice and give Him glory, for the marriage of the Lamb has come, and His wife has made herself ready." And to her it was granted to be arrayed in fine linen, clean and bright, for the fine linen is the righteous acts of the saints.
>
> **REVELATION 19:6-8**

At this point, the marriage supper of the Lamb has taken place, and the betrothed bride of Christ is now referred to as "His wife," to whom it was granted to be arrayed in the garments worn by the armies in heaven who return with Christ. For this to happen, the bride, or the church, must have already been raptured to heaven earlier in order to return with the Lord.

This moment in time is both part of and the end of the seventieth seven. It is at this point that the one-third of the Jews who survived the tribulation will see Jesus for who He is: "I will pour on the house of David and on the inhabitants of Jerusalem the Spirit of grace and supplication; then they will look on Me whom they pierced. Yes, they will mourn for Him as one mourns for his only son, and grieve for Him as one grieves for a firstborn" (Zechariah 12:10).

Second Corinthians 7:10 says that "godly sorrow produces repentance leading to salvation," and that is what we see pictured in Zechariah 12:10—the repentance of the remnant of Jews for piercing their Messiah. They will experience a deep grief like that of a family mourning the loss of an only son.

Zechariah also gives us some interesting details in a couple other favorite passages related to the second coming:

> Then the Lord will go forth and fight against those nations,
> as He fights in the day of battle.

ZECHARIAH 14:3

> This shall be the plague with which the Lord will strike
> all the people who fought against Jerusalem:
> Their flesh shall dissolve while they stand on their feet,
> their eyes shall dissolve in their sockets,
> and their tongues shall dissolve in their mouths.

ZECHARIAH 14:12

The verses that follow address events that will take place during the millennium, which assures us that the above passages are related to the battle that ends the tribulation, when Jesus comes back with the armies of heaven. He will fight "as He fights" in the day of battle. If we want to know how He fights, we need look no further than the plagues in Egypt: water turned to blood, the Egyptians had boils on their skin, great hailstones came down, and locusts ravaged the land. These are the weapons at the Lord's disposal. Just as a side note, there are some who believe that nuclear exchanges may be evident in Zechariah 14:12 in relation to people's flesh and eyes dissolving. The Lord fights with weapons that are far more powerful than man's puny (by comparison) nuclear weapons. For example:

> Have you entered the treasury of snow, or have you seen the treasury of hail, which I have reserved for the time of trouble, for the day of battle and war?
>
> JOB 38:22-23

> Great hail from heaven fell upon men, each hailstone about the weight of a talent. Men blasphemed God because of the plague of the hail, since that plague was exceedingly great.
>
> REVELATION 16:21

> I will bring him to judgment with pestilence and bloodshed; I will rain down on him, on his troops, and on the many peoples who are with him, flooding rain, great hailstones, fire, and brimstone. Thus I will magnify Myself and sanctify Myself, and I will be known in the eyes of many nations. Then they shall know that I am the LORD.
>
> EZEKIEL 38:22-23

A talent of silver weighs around 100 pounds, and a talent of gold around 200 pounds. This is the kind of hail God has stored in His treasury "for the time of trouble." This is how God will end the Eze-kiel war. He will fight in that day as He fights in the day of battle.

There are those who are not comfortable with the picture of Jesus presented in Revelation 19. They prefer the meek and mild "lamb across the shoulders" Jesus we see portrayed in art. But in our journey through the last days, we have seen that man will become more aggressively rebellious against God, and judgment will be the only way to stop the moral and spiritual slide that has now escalated to a freefall into delusion. It is interesting to consider that part of the reason Jesus was rejected by the Jews at His first coming is because they wanted a conquering rider on a white horse, not a lamb to take away their sins. Today, many people don't want a Jesus who is judge of all the earth, but a Jesus who is accepting of anything and everything people want to be and do. But Jesus has to be both Savior and judge, because unless we are cleansed by His shed blood, we cannot be reconciled to God and thus qualified to ride on white horses with Him at His return.

Jesus has to be both Savior and judge, because unless we are cleansed by His shed blood, we cannot be reconciled to God and thus qualified to ride on white horses with Him at His return.

The prophet Isaiah depicted Jesus in His fullness:

Unto us a Child is born,
unto us a Son is given;
and the government will be upon His shoulder.
And His name will be called
Wonderful, Counselor, Mighty God,

Everlasting Father, Prince of Peace.
Of the increase of His government and peace
there will be no end,
upon the throne of David and over His kingdom,
to order it and establish it with judgment and justice
from that time forward, even forever.
The zeal of the LORD of hosts will perform this.

ISAIAH 9:6-7

The Child was born and a Son was given; the government has yet to be on His shoulder. This is what the second coming is all about. The Lord Jesus will take on the role of world ruler and shoulder the responsibility of reigning in righteousness from David's throne. He will assume all governmental authority and oversee justice on the earth. The Prince of Peace will bring about a world peace that has never been experienced, and He will bring back to the world an environment that hasn't existed since the early days of man.

In that day His feet will stand on the Mount of Olives,
which faces Jerusalem on the east.
And the Mount of Olives shall be split in two,
from east to west,
making a very large valley;
half of the mountain shall move toward the north
and half of it toward the south.

ZECHARIAH 14:4

In that day it shall be
that living waters shall flow from Jerusalem,
half of them toward the eastern sea
and half of them toward the western sea;
in both summer and winter it shall occur.

And the LORD shall be King over all the earth.
In that day it shall be—
"The LORD is one,"
and His name one.

ZECHARIAH 14:8-9

In the next chapter, we will talk more about what the earth will be like during the millennium. But here, we see pictured an instantaneous transition when Jesus' feet touch down on the Mount of Olives. Living waters will flow from the mountain, restoring life to the oceans of the world, including the Dead Sea. Remember, during the tribulation, every living thing in the sea died at the pouring out of the second bowl of God's undiluted wrath in Revelation 16:3.

This peace that only the Lord can bring is the end result of Him engaging His enemies in battle and soundly defeating those who gathered in battle against Him. Just as the Lord brought plagues upon Pharaoh and the Egyptians for refusing to let His people go and worship Him, at the end of the Ezekiel war, God will pour out His wrath against Israel's enemies.

The Egyptians shall know that I am the LORD, when I stretch out My hand on Egypt and bring out the children of Israel from among them.

EXODUS 7:5

"I will make My holy name known in the midst of My people Israel, and I will not let them profane My holy name anymore. Then the nations shall know that I am the LORD, the Holy One in Israel. Surely it is coming, and it shall be done," says the Lord GOD. "This is the day of which I have spoken."

EZEKIEL 39:7-8

It has been estimated that since the birth of the church in AD 32, more than 70 million Christians have been martyred for their faith.[3] The most deadly century since the time of Jesus was the twentieth century, during which, according to Christianity.com, more than 26 million Christians are said to have been killed for their belief in Jesus.[4] And many believers will be killed during the tribulation as well:

> When He opened the fifth seal, I saw under the altar the souls of those who had been slain for the word of God and for the testimony which they held. And they cried with a loud voice, saying, "How long, O Lord, holy and true, until You judge and avenge our blood on those who dwell on the earth?" Then a white robe was given to each of them; and it was said to them that they should rest a little while longer, until both the number of their fellow servants and their brethren, who would be killed as they were, was completed.
>
> REVELATION 6:9-11

As John 5:22 says, all judgment has been committed to the Son. At His return, He will be clothed with a robe dipped in blood, and it is He who will tread the winepress of Almighty God's wrath. He will answer the prayers of the tribulation martyrs and those who, through the ages, have similarly prayed, "How long, O Lord, until you avenge our blood on a ruthless world?"

While there are many people who are more comfortable with Jesus as He was in the manger or nailed to the cross as the lamb of God, Scripture makes it clear this same Jesus will judge in righteousness and war against His enemies. He will fight with all the weapons of heaven at His disposal.

> Another angel came out of the temple which is in heaven, he also having a sharp sickle. And another angel came

out from the altar, who had power over fire, and he cried with a loud cry to him who had the sharp sickle, saying, "Thrust in your sharp sickle and gather the clusters of the vine of the earth, for her grapes are fully ripe." So the angel thrust his sickle into the earth and gathered the vine of the earth, and threw it into the great winepress of the wrath of God. And the winepress was trampled outside the city, and blood came out of the winepress, up to the horses' bridles, for one thousand six hundred furlongs.

REVELATION 14:17-20

The sixth angel poured out his bowl on the great river Euphrates, and its water was dried up, so that the way of the kings from the east might be prepared. And I saw three unclean spirits like frogs coming out of the mouth of the dragon, out of the mouth of the beast, and out of the mouth of the false prophet. For they are spirits of demons, performing signs, which go out to the kings of the earth and of the whole world, to gather them to the battle of that great day of God Almighty.

"Behold, I am coming as a thief. Blessed is he who watches, and keeps his garments, lest he walk naked and they see his shame." And they gathered them together to the place called in Hebrew, Armageddon.

REVELATION 16:12-16

Revelation 19 tells us that Jesus, who will return on a white horse, will tread the winepress of God's wrath, and His garments will be sprinkled with blood. The distance of 1,600 furlongs is the distance from Dan to Beersheba, or the length of the country of Israel. While many see China as being represented in the phrase "the kings from the east," we need to remember that Israel's ancient enemies dwelled in lands east of the Euphrates. According to Exodus 23:31, the eastern boundary of Israel is the Euphrates River. This area would include ancient Babylon and Persia (Iran), and of course Turkey, where the headwaters of the Euphrates are formed. We also need to keep in mind that during the tribulation, the geopolitical landscape of the entire world will change, and all nations will be under the rule of the antichrist and his cronies. So "the kings from the east" does not have to refer to China—it could refer to the areas east of the Euphrates River that have always been problematic for Israel.

Whoever the kings of the east are, they will meet their demise at the hands of the Lion of Judah during the battle of that great day of God Almighty. It is this battle and the return of Jesus to Jerusalem—specifically to the Mount of Olives—that will allow the world to experience true peace, true justice, and absolute righteousness because the one who will rule after that battle is true and righteous.

Though God waits patiently for people to repent, many won't:

> The Lord is not slack concerning His promise, as some count slackness, but is longsuffering toward us, not willing that any should perish but that all should come to repentance.

> **2 PETER 3:9**

> The rest of mankind, who were not killed by these plagues, did not repent of the works of their hands, that they should not worship demons, and idols of gold, silver, brass, stone, and wood, which can neither see nor hear nor walk. And they did not repent of their murders or their sorceries or their sexual immorality or their thefts.

> **REVELATION 9:20-21**

Revelation 16:9 and 16:11 record the same lack of repentance on the part of the earth dwellers even when they know they are experiencing the wrath of Almighty God. There is a belligerence in today's world that can only be compared to that of the days of Noah. Remember that Noah took 120 years to build the ark on dry ground on a planet that had never seen rain (Genesis 2:5). During this time, Noah preached righteousness (2 Peter 2:5), and yet mankind was completely indifferent to the clear signs that judgment was coming. We are living in days like those of Noah. Many people don't care what God has said and become angry and even violent at the mention of God's standards and man's violation of them. Things will get so bad on the earth that only God's wrath will stop ruthless, godless humanity from destroying everyone and everything that stands in its way.

> Why do the nations rage,
> and the people plot a vain thing?
> The kings of the earth set themselves,
> and the rulers take counsel together,
> against the LORD and against His Anointed, saying,
> "Let us break Their bonds in pieces
> and cast away Their cords from us."
>
> He who sits in the heavens shall laugh;
> the Lord shall hold them in derision.
> Then He shall speak to them in His wrath,
> and distress them in His deep displeasure.
>
> **PSALM 2:1-5**

In response to the vain plots of the people of the earth, Jesus will break the nations with a rod of iron and dash them to pieces like a potter's vessel. He will have done everything necessary to save them, including shedding His blood for them. Yet in the end, even in the midst of the catastrophic wrath of God, they will deny Him and worship the dragon instead. The only thing that will stop people is the wrath of Almighty God.

After that, Jesus will sit on the throne of David and rule in absolute righteousness. This will be a time with no elections, no broken campaign promises, no exploitation of the masses for personal gain, no political corruption. There will be no competing religions, and no more wars (at least not until the end of the millennium). When will this happen, and how long will it last? It will happen after the second coming of Jesus, and it will last for 1,000 years.

CHAPTER 10

THE MILLENNIUM

Before we jump into the specifics about the millennial reign of Christ on earth, we need to do a bit more interpretive housekeeping and answer a question posed by many regarding Daniel 12:11-12:

> From the time that the daily sacrifice is taken away, and the abomination of desolation is set up, there shall be one thousand two hundred and ninety days. Blessed is he who waits, and comes to the one thousand three hundred and thirty-five days.

In Daniel and Revelation, we are told multiple times and in various ways that the duration of the tribulation is two 42-month periods of 30-day months, or two 1,260-day periods. This makes the entire tribulation 2,520 days long, or 84 30-day months, equaling seven years. This seven-year period is the final week of the 70 weeks prophesied in Daniel 9. So why does Daniel 12 mention 1,290 days, and 1,335 days?

The 1,290-day number reveals that 30 days before the abomination of desolation takes place at the midpoint of the tribulation, the antichrist will take away the Jews' right to offer sacrifices at the temple.

Thirty days after he does this, he will declare that he is God. And 1,260 days after that, Jesus will return to the earth. Again, in reverse, 1,290 days before Jesus comes again, the daily sacrifices will be halted, and 30 days later, the antichrist will claim to be God. That's the reason for the 1,290-day number.

What about the 1,335-day number and the blessing promised to those who make it to that day? This additional 75 days is most likely the time during which the sheep and the goats are divided:

> When the Son of Man comes in His glory, and all the holy angels with Him, then He will sit on the throne of His glory. All the nations will be gathered before Him, and He will separate them one from another, as a shepherd divides his sheep from the goats. And He will set the sheep on His right hand, but the goats on the left. Then the King will say to those on His right hand, "Come, you blessed of My Father, inherit the kingdom prepared for you from the foundation of the world: for I was hungry and you gave Me food; I was thirsty and you gave Me drink; I was a stranger and you took Me in; I was naked and you clothed Me; I was sick and you visited Me; I was in prison and you came to Me."
>
> MATTHEW 25:31-36

The sheep, the blessed ones of the two groups, will then inquire of the Lord when they did the things He commended them for. And He will answer, "Inasmuch as you did it to one of the least of these My brethren, you did it to Me" (verse 40).

> Then He will also say to those on the left hand, "Depart from Me, you cursed, into the everlasting fire prepared for the devil and his angels: for I was hungry and you gave Me

no food; I was thirsty and you gave Me no drink; I was a
stranger and you did not take Me in, naked and you did
not clothe Me, sick and in prison and you did not visit Me."
Then they also will answer Him, saying, "Lord, when did
we see You hungry or thirsty or a stranger or naked or sick
or in prison, and did not minister to You?" Then He will
answer them, saying, "Assuredly, I say to you, inasmuch
as you did not do it to one of the least of these, you did
not do it to Me." And these will go away into everlasting
punishment, but the righteous into eternal life.

MATTHEW 25:41-46

Daniel 12:2 also tells us that at the time of Christ's return, the dead
bodies of believing Jews will experience what the dead in Christ did
at the rapture: a physical resurrection. The reason we need to note
this, beyond explaining the extra 75 days in Daniel 12, is that it tells
us that everyone who enters into the millennium will be a believer.
This will help us in our understanding of why a rebellion will occur
at the end of the millennium. After all, every person who enters the
millennium will be a believer, and Christ will rule in absolute perfection during the 1,000 years. And yet, at the end of the millennium,
many will turn against the Lord.

Of the many questions related to Bible prophecy, most begin with
what? Or *when?* Questions about the millennium often include *why?*
Why is it that, after the seventieth seven, and after church-age believers as well as the Old Testament and tribulation saints have received
their glorified bodies, we have to come back to earth not only at all,
but for 1,000 years?

Some have offered the solution that the millennium is not literal but figurative. They say there will be no actual millennium in
which Jesus rules the earth and the glorified saints rule with Him.
Still others say we are already in the millennium, or that Jesus can't

come back and begin the millennium until the church has dominion over the world.

What does Scripture say? Is the millennium an actual future time period? Will we literally return with Jesus, and will He rule the world from David's throne? The answer to all of these questions is yes! How do we know?

> I saw an angel coming down from heaven, having the key to the bottomless pit and a great chain in his hand. He laid hold of the dragon, that serpent of old, who is the Devil and Satan, and bound him for a thousand years; and he cast him into the bottomless pit, and shut him up, and set a seal on him, so that he should deceive the nations no more till the thousand years were finished. But after these things he must be released for a little while.

> And I saw thrones, and they sat on them, and judgment was committed to them. Then I saw the souls of those who had been beheaded for their witness to Jesus and for the word of God, who had not worshiped the beast or his image, and had not received his mark on their foreheads or on their hands. And they lived and reigned with Christ for a thousand years. But the rest of the dead did not live again until the thousand years were finished. This is the first resurrection. Blessed and holy is he who has part in the first resurrection. Over such the second death has no power, but they shall be priests of God and of Christ, and shall reign with Him a thousand years.

> Now when the thousand years have expired, Satan will be released from his prison and will go out to deceive the nations which are in the four corners of the earth, Gog

and Magog, to gather them together to battle, whose number is as the sand of the sea.

REVELATION 20:1-8

The Greek word *chilioi*, which translates to "a thousand," is used six times in Revelation 20, and is found 11 times in the New Testament. Every single time, the word is used in a literal sense. The one time the word is used in an illustration, it still carries a literal meaning: "Beloved, do not forget this one thing, that with the Lord one day is as a thousand years, and a thousand years as one day" (2 Peter 3:8).

Peter was making the point that God dwells outside of time. He was not establishing an equation to calculate the approximate timing of the rapture or the duration of time before the millennium. The "thousand years"/"one day" comparison he made would have to be understood as literal to make any sense. This and the other usages of *chilioi* establish that the only way to interpret the term is literally. So yes, the 1,000 years is literal and not figurative.

Because we know the millennium is literal and is preceded by the seventieth seven (the tribulation), we know that it's not the church's dominion over the world that will usher in the millennium, for two reasons: (1) the content of our last chapter, and (2) the church's absence during the tribulation. The church does not need to and will not have dominion over the world before Jesus can rule over it. Jesus is going to rule the world because He is God, not because the church made it ready for Him by taking dominion over it.

> Jesus is going to rule the world because He is God, not because the church made it ready for Him by taking dominion over it.

Now let's move on to the big question, and then we'll address specifics about this 1,000-year time period: Why? What is the purpose of the millennium? The Bible says nothing about the why of the millennium. However, as we glance back through history, we can make a calculated speculation as to why God would want to bring about a millennial kingdom after the church has already been in heaven, after the Old Testament saints have been resurrected, and after the Jews who survived the tribulation have all come to faith in Jesus as their Messiah.

In the garden, when God created man in His own image and took out of the man what He fashioned into a woman, He gave them one command, and they broke it. Sin and death entered into the world. After that, God left no further instructions or restrictions other than telling the first couple that the once-perfect world was now imperfect. In less than 2,000 years, man, left to his own devices, became so corrupt that God was sorry that He had made him (Genesis 6:6). He then destroyed every living thing with a global flood, except for those who boarded the ark.

Afterward, God promised to never flood the earth again and gave the world a "sign of the covenant" He had made with mankind and all the earth's living creatures, and He "set [His] rainbow in the cloud" (Genesis 9:12-13). This signified God's promise to never again flood the entire earth. Within a relatively short time, man's response was to build a tower at Babel (later called Babylon) to reach the heavens, and idolatry was born. In response, the Lord "confused the language of all the earth" and scattered the people abroad everywhere (Genesis 11:9).

After God took preventative steps to keep the people of the world from unifying against Him instead of being united in Him, He selected a single group of people to whom He would commit His oracles and for whom He would give a law to make their lives pleasing to Him and better for themselves. He called a man named Abram out of the pagan Ur of the Chaldees, and gave him these promises:

> The LORD had said to Abram:
> "Get out of your country,
> from your family
> and from your father's house,
> to a land that I will show you.
> I will make you a great nation;
> I will bless you
> and make your name great;
> and you shall be a blessing.
> I will bless those who bless you,
> and I will curse him who curses you;
> and in you all the families of the earth shall be blessed."
>
> **GENESIS 12:1-3**

From Abram would come the Israelites to whom God would give all the land of Canaan, and through whom the Messiah, who would be a blessing to all the families of the earth, would come.

Yet by the time the one who would bless all the families of the earth came, the Israelites had replaced much of God's laws with their own teachings. And they rejected the one whom they had been waiting for, condemning Him to the cross as a blasphemer who made Himself equal with God by claiming to be God's Son (John 5:18).

After Christ was despised and rejected by the very people He came from in order to save them from their sins, the plan of God then focused on the Gentiles (and by comparison, a small number of Jews). Those who believed in Him were given the Holy Spirit to guide and direct them, and to guarantee their future inheritance (Ephesians 1:13-14). These people comprise the church. To the church,

God gave apostles and prophets as a foundation to build on (Ephesians 2:20), and He gave evangelists, pastors, and teachers to equip people for the work of ministry (Ephesians 4:11-12). And given time, where do things end up? Right back where they started:

> As the days of Noah were, so also will the coming of the Son of Man be. For as in the days before the flood, they were eating and drinking, marrying and giving in marriage, until the day that Noah entered the ark, and did not know until the flood came and took them all away, so also will the coming of the Son of Man be.
>
> MATTHEW 24:37-39

In Noah's day, man was indifferent to the clear signs of impending judgment and had a cavalier, business-as-usual attitude in response to God's warnings, which were communicated through Noah's building of an ark. Jesus said that in the last days, it will be as it was in the days of Noah, and indeed it is.

So what is the purpose of the millennium? Here is my calculated speculation: God created man perfectly, and man chose death and imperfection over obedience and perfection. The world has been a mess ever since. God left man on his own in the sense of allowing him to do what he pleased, and man became so corrupt that God sent the flood, destroyed the wicked, and started over with eight righteous people.

After having left man to his own inclinations, God then gave man a law to follow and promised a redeemer who would repair what was broken in the garden. Man violated the law and killed the redeemer when He came. The redeemer rose from the dead, gave His Spirit to those who believed in Him, and empowered them to be His witnesses. Two thousand years later, things are once again as they were in the days of Noah.

My opinion is that the possible purpose of the millennium is that corruption has ruled the earth since the fall of man, and the world has never been run right. The millennium will be a time during which the perfect one Himself will rule the nations in righteousness. At the end of the 1,000 years, Satan will be released for a short time, and countless people from all over the world will side with the devil and fight against the King of kings and His people, but they will not prevail.

I believe we could argue that the millennium justifies the great white throne judgment because by that time, God will have come at man from every direction in the hopes of saving his soul. And yet massive numbers of people—after having seen for 1,000 years how the world *should* be run—will still reject God and choose Satan. Thus, what happens at the great white throne is completely justified.

This is an opinion as to why there will be a millennium. I will also add this: Even if this is not the reason, there will still be a millennial kingdom. Now, before we move to the *what* question— that is, what will the world be like during the millennium—we must address a second *why* for the millennium: It's because there are unfulfilled promises and prophecies that will be fulfilled during that time.

One prophecy that still remains unfulfilled is that Israel has never possessed all the land that God gave to them as an inheritance:

> On the same day the LORD made a covenant with Abram, saying: "To your descendants I have given this land, from the river of Egypt to the great river, the River Euphrates—the Kenites, the Kenezzites, the Kadmonites, the Hittites, the Perizzites, the Rephaim, the Amorites, the Canaanites, the Girgashites, and the Jebusites"
>
> **GENESIS 15:18-21**

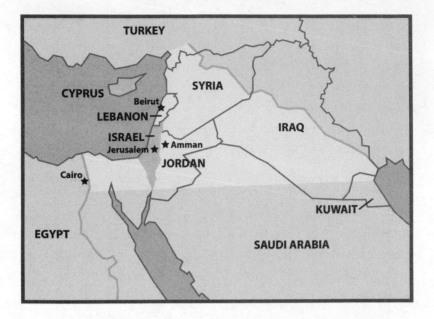

The map above shows the land that modern Israel now inhabits, and you can see how far short it is of all the land that God promised, which is shown in the lightest areas on the map. King Solomon occupied the greatest portion of the land promised to Israel, but even during his day, the borders fell well short of all that God had promised.

Here's another prophecy that is still largely unfulfilled:

> Unto us a Child is born,
> unto us a Son is given;
> and the government will be upon His shoulder.
> And His name will be called
> Wonderful, Counselor, Mighty God,
> Everlasting Father, Prince of Peace.
> Of the increase of His government and peace
> there will be no end,
> upon the throne of David and over His kingdom,
> to order it and establish it with judgment and justice

from that time forward, even forever.
The zeal of the LORD of hosts will perform this.

ISAIAH 9:6-7

The majority of this prophecy has yet to be fulfilled, and if is not fulfilled, we have to ask: Are there others that will not be? That's not a road we would want to go down, and thankfully, we don't need to. During the millennium, the responsibility of governing the earth will fall solely on Jesus' shoulders, and it will stay that way forever. The "throne of David" in Isaiah 9:7 speaks of the throne of human government, so this passage cannot be applied to the heavenly realm, for the throne of David is not in heaven. The prophet Isaiah reveals the identity of this world ruler as the Child and the Son given, who is, among other things, the Prince of Peace.

During the millennium, the responsibility of governing the earth will fall solely on Jesus' shoulders, and it will stay that way forever.

Israel has yet to occupy all the land promised to them by God, and Jesus—the Prince of Peace—has yet to rule from David's throne in Jerusalem. This is part of why the millennium must happen.

There is one more *why* detail we should look at before we explore *what* the millennium will be like. Many people ask, "Why will there be sacrifices during the millennium? Didn't Jesus die as the perfect sacrifice 'once for all,' as Hebrews 7:27 says?"

There are multiple passages that say there will be sacrifices during the millennium, including Isaiah 56:6-8, Jeremiah 33:15-19, and Zechariah 14:16. The most significant passage regarding this is also the one that details the size and scope of the millennial temple, which will be far greater than the other two that have existed. Ezekiel chapters 43–46 give us a vivid description of the sacrifices that will be offered in this magnificent temple.

Now, here is what troubles many believers: Hebrews 10:4 clearly says, "It is not possible that the blood of bulls and goats could take away sins." If it was not possible for the blood of bulls and goats to take away sins before the millennium, then it is not possible for the blood of bulls and goats to take away sin during the millennium. The sacrifices that will be offered during the millennium will be given for the same reason they were offered during the Old Testament era: as a reminder of the great cost associated with covering sin, and of the necessity of innocent blood to pay the price. In Old Testament times, people looked forward to when a perfect sacrifice would be offered in the person of Christ. In the millennium, people will look back on when the perfect sacrifice was offered in Christ. The sacrifices during the millennium will be memorial tributes to the death of the Lamb of God, who came to take away the sins of the world.

> It shall come to pass that everyone who is left of all the nations which came against Jerusalem shall go up from year to year to worship the King, the LORD of hosts, and to keep the Feast of Tabernacles.
>
> ZECHARIAH 14:16

Again, this is part of the biblical *why* for the millennium. Jesus fulfilled the Passover, the Feast of Unleavened Bread, and the Feast of First Fruits at His first coming; and Pentecost was fulfilled when the church was born. The Feast of Trumpets will be fulfilled at His second coming and the Day of Atonement at the dividing of the sheep and goats, which will take place after the seventieth seven. And as

Zechariah 14:16 says, the Feast of Tabernacles will be fulfilled by the millennium.

Now that we've addressed some of the *whys* of the millennium, let's look at *what* the world will be like.

> The wolf also shall dwell with the lamb,
> the leopard shall lie down with the young goat,
> the calf and the young lion and the fatling together;
> and a little child shall lead them.
> The cow and the bear shall graze;
> their young ones shall lie down together;
> and the lion shall eat straw like the ox.
> The nursing child shall play by the cobra's hole,
> and the weaned child shall put his hand in the viper's den.
> They shall not hurt nor destroy in all My holy mountain,
> for the earth shall be full of the knowledge of the LORD
> as the waters cover the sea.
>
> And in that day there shall be a Root of Jesse,
> who shall stand as a banner to the people;
> for the Gentiles shall seek Him,
> and His resting place shall be glorious.

ISAIAH 11:6-10

The best way to describe the physical aspects of the millennium is that the earth will return to an Eden-like condition. The enmity between the animal kingdom and humanity will be reversed. The whole world will know of the Lord, and the Lord Himself—the root of Jesse (King David's father)—will rule and reign from His temple in Jerusalem.

> In that day there will be an altar to the LORD in the midst
> of the land of Egypt, and a pillar to the LORD at its border.

And it will be for a sign and for a witness to the LORD of hosts in the land of Egypt; for they will cry to the LORD because of the oppressors, and He will send them a Savior and a Mighty One, and He will deliver them. Then the LORD will be known to Egypt, and the Egyptians will know the LORD in that day, and will make sacrifice and offering; yes, they will make a vow to the LORD and perform it. And the LORD will strike Egypt, He will strike and heal it; they will return to the LORD, and He will be entreated by them and heal them.

In that day there will be a highway from Egypt to Assyria, and the Assyrian will come into Egypt and the Egyptian into Assyria, and the Egyptians will serve with the Assyrians.

In that day Israel will be one of three with Egypt and Assyria—a blessing in the midst of the land, whom the LORD of hosts shall bless, saying, "Blessed is Egypt My people, and Assyria the work of My hands, and Israel My inheritance."

ISAIAH 19:19-25

During the millennium, the Egyptians and the Assyrians, former enemies and captors of Israel, will be one with Israel, and the religious and ethnic tensions that caused wars and invasions throughout the previous millennia will end. People will know the Lord of hosts. Yet another aspect of the millennium will be the long life spans:

No more shall an infant from there live but a few days,
nor an old man who has not fulfilled his days;
for the child shall die one hundred years old,
but the sinner being one hundred years old shall be accursed.

ISAIAH 65:20

We need to remember that everyone who enters the millennium will be believers, but not all will be glorified human beings. The life spans people knew during the days prior to the flood will return to being the norm, and people will live for hundreds of years. If someone dies at 100 years of age, it will be like as if a child had died. We can also see that sin will be present on the earth during the millennium, and this will underscore the fact that there are unglorified human beings who continue to procreate and give birth to children who, like all of humanity, must decide to be for or against the King of kings and Lord of lords who rules the earth in righteousness from Jerusalem.

> It shall come to pass that everyone who is left of all the nations which came against Jerusalem shall go up from year to year to worship the King, the LORD of hosts, and to keep the Feast of Tabernacles. And it shall be that whichever of the families of the earth do not come up to Jerusalem to worship the King, the LORD of hosts, on them there will be no rain. If the family of Egypt will not come up and enter in, they shall have no rain; they shall receive the plague with which the LORD strikes the nations who do not come up to keep the Feast of Tabernacles. This shall be the punishment of Egypt and the punishment of all the nations that do not come up to keep the Feast of Tabernacles.
>
> ZECHARIAH 14:16-19

We will talk more about this in the next chapter, but here again, we find that even with the perfect physical environment that will exist during the millennium, and with the gracious and loving King of kings ruling righteously over the world, some will still refuse to send representatives to celebrate the Feast of Tabernacles. In doing this, they will bring punishment upon themselves. The observing of the Feast of Tabernacles will be a sign of unity with Christ and His reign and will be commemorated by those who were identified as sheep in Matthew 25:31-46. These sheep will have been separated from the goats based on their treatment of the Jews during the reign of the antichrist. The sheep will enter into the millennium, and they will enjoy the blessings and benefits of the Eden-like conditions on the earth, including an extended life span.

The millennium is not heaven on earth. Rather, it is 1,000 years of a perfect God, along with His perfected people, ruling over a near-perfect earth filled with imperfect people, including some who refuse to honor and obey Him even in the midst of near-perfect circumstances.

> Now it shall come to pass in the latter days
> that the mountain of the LORD's house
> shall be established on the top of the mountains,
> and shall be exalted above the hills;
> and peoples shall flow to it.
> Many nations shall come and say,
> "Come, and let us go up to the mountain of the LORD,
> to the house of the God of Jacob;
> He will teach us His ways,
> and we shall walk in His paths."
> For out of Zion the law shall go forth,
> and the word of the LORD from Jerusalem.
> He shall judge between many peoples,
> and rebuke strong nations afar off;
> they shall beat their swords into plowshares,
> and their spears into pruning hooks;
> nation shall not lift up sword against nation,
> neither shall they learn war anymore.

But everyone shall sit under his vine and under his fig tree,
and no one shall make them afraid;
for the mouth of the LORD of hosts has spoken.

MICAH 4:1-4

A near-perfect earth, a fair and righteous government and rulers, long life spans, no enmity with the animal kingdom, global peace and unity, no war, no fear, and no famine—and yet some will say there is no need to observe the Feast of Tabernacles. This helps to explain a key *why* of the millennium. It doesn't matter what God does to draw people to Himself. Some people will still reject Him and do what they want to do, and the millennium will confirm that.

The millennium is going to be an amazing time for the earth and its inhabitants. Sadly, however, it will not end as well as it begins.

CHAPTER 11

THE FINAL WAR

The Bible is filled with shocking and surprising incidents, many of which document the wrongful behavior of God's people. Abram lying about Sarah not being his wife and claiming she was his sister is one example. He did this in an effort to protect himself. Even so, the Bible describes Abraham as "a friend of God." Another example is when the Israelites longed to return to Egypt even after 430 years of bondage in slavery, and even after the people saw the mighty hand of God deliver them. Yet these are the chosen people of God. Startling accounts like these pepper the pages of Scripture, and perhaps one of the most shocking of all is what will happen after Christ has ruled justly and fairly for 1,000 years in a world of bounty and beauty:

When the thousand years have expired, Satan will be released from his prison and will go out to deceive the nations which are in the four corners of the earth, Gog and Magog, to gather them together to battle, whose number is as the sand of the sea. They went up on the breadth of the earth and surrounded the camp of the saints and the beloved city. And fire came down from God out of heaven and devoured them. The devil, who deceived them, was cast into the lake of fire and brimstone where the beast

and the false prophet are. And they will be tormented day
and night forever and ever.

REVELATION 20:7-10

Again, a bit of doctrinal housekeeping is in order here. Note that
at the conclusion of this battle, Satan will be cast into the lake of fire,
where the beast and false prophet "are," not "were." There are some
today who teach a doctrine called annihilationism, which basically
says that the lake of fire will consume all the unbelieving dead, and
as a result, they will cease to exist. Some say this will happen after the
great white throne judgment. But Revelation 20:10 exposes a problem with that doctrine: When Satan is cast into the lake of fire, the
beast and false prophet will still be there, even after having already
been there for 1,000 years. This is the same lake of fire unbelievers
will be cast into after the great white throne judgment. If this fire is
supposed to consume those who are cast into it, then how is it that
the beast and false prophet survive for 1,000 years?

Let's go back to what happens at the end of the tribulation:

> The beast was captured, and with him the false prophet
> who worked signs in his presence, by which he deceived
> those who received the mark of the beast and those who
> worshiped his image. These two were cast alive into the
> lake of fire burning with brimstone.

REVELATION 19:20

After the beast and false prophet are thrown into the lake of fire,
Satan will be bound for 1,000 years (Revelation 20:1-2). Then according to Revelation 20:10, at the end of the 1,000 years, Satan will join
the beast and false prophet in the lake of fire, where they have been
for the duration of the millennium. This pretty much annihilates
the annihilist position.

As we saw in the last chapter, no matter what God does, it won't be good enough for some people. Here's the scenario during the millennium: Satan has been bound, unable to tempt mankind with his devices. The King of all kings will rule over the earth for 1,000 years. Judgment will be fair, and justice will be served in every way possible, for Christ's kingdom will have come to earth, and His will is going to be done on earth as it is in heaven.

Yet at the first chance to rebel against the perfect rule of the King of kings and Prince of Peace, billions will side with the devil and surround Jerusalem in an effort to overthrow Christ and seize the city.

Back in chapter 6, when we learned about the Ezekiel war, we noted that Gog and Magog would appear on the pages of Scripture once again at the end of the millennium. As noted there, it is possible that this phrase refers to enemies of Israel.

Here, we'll find it helpful to look at Daniel 10, where Daniel had a disturbing vision that he knew was true, and yet it caused him to fast and mourn for three weeks because of what was coming. He had prayed, yet no answer had come. And then this happened:

> On the twenty-fourth day of the first month, as I was by the side of the great river, that is, the Tigris, I lifted my eyes and looked, and behold, a certain man clothed in linen, whose waist was girded with gold of Uphaz! His body was like beryl, his face like the appearance of lightning, his eyes like torches of fire, his arms and feet like burnished bronze in color, and the sound of his words like the voice of a multitude.
>
> DANIEL 10:4-6

Daniel has a troubling vision, and the text implies that three weeks after his time of fasting and mourning, he has an encounter with a being who is clearly an angel. The angel touches Daniel and pulls back the curtain on the realm of the supernatural and says to him,

> Do not fear, Daniel, for from the first day that you set your
> heart to understand, and to humble yourself before your
> God, your words were heard; and I have come because
> of your words. But the prince of the kingdom of Persia
> withstood me twenty-one days; and behold, Michael, one
> of the chief princes, came to help me, for I had been left
> alone there with the kings of Persia.

DANIEL 10:12-13

In this passage, Daniel reveals to us that within the angelic realm of "good guys and bad guys" (faithful angels and fallen angels), there are specific assignments given to some of these angels. "The prince of the kingdom of Persia" is identified as one who stands in opposition to the King of kings, and Michael is identified as one of the "chief princes" of the heavenly realm.

Therefore, it is possible that Gog is the name of a fallen angel assigned to lead the enemy forces against Jerusalem. This would explain how he can be present in the Ezekiel war scenario more than 1,000 years earlier and again at the end of the 1,000-year reign of Christ. Magog is located in the mountainous region between Cappadocia and Media. Cappadocia is in modern-day Turkey, and Media is the Kurdish region at the northwest corner of Iran, home of the Persians. Media was home to the Medes, whose descendants are the Kurds. Modern Cappadocia and Kurdistan were both within the boundaries of the ancient Medo-Persian Empire, which conquered the Babylonians.

This creates a second link to the possibility that Gog is the name of a fallen angel, much like we know Satan's name is Lucifer. God's messenger angel is Gabriel, and Michael, whose name means "who is like God?,'" is an archangel. So whether Gog speaks figuratively of Israel's enemies or it is the name of a fallen angel who leads the armies of the world in an effort to overthrown the King of kings and Lord of lords, the fact remains that no matter what God does, it will never be enough for some people. God's grace and the hardness of man's heart are seen side by side in John 3:

> God so loved the world that He gave His only begotten Son, that whoever believes in Him should not perish but have everlasting life. For God did not send His Son into the world to condemn the world, but that the world through Him might be saved.
>
> He who believes in Him is not condemned; but he who does not believe is condemned already, because he has not believed in the name of the only begotten Son of God. And this is the condemnation, that the light has come into the world, and men loved darkness rather than light, because their deeds were evil.
>
> JOHN 3:16-19

While history has proven the hardness of man's heart, it will be proven once again when the nations who join with Gog and Magog—whose numbers are as the sand of the sea—come against God. Consider what Jeremiah wrote about the condition of the human heart: "The heart is deceitful above all things, and desperately wicked; who can know it? I, the LORD, search the heart, I test the mind, even to give every man according to his ways, according to the fruit of his doings" (Jeremiah 17:9-10).

We live in a time where, in some places, it is supposedly a hate crime to say that men can't have babies, or that there are only two genders, or that you can't decide your gender, or it is genetically and biologically determined. We have just come through a season during which we heard people say, almost daily, "Trust the science," yet these same people deny the science and can't even define what a woman is.

We live in a time when the most vulnerable and helpless among us are murdered by the millions, and abortion is the number one cause of human death globally.[5] We live in an age where elections are nothing but mudslinging contests in which candidates do little to promote themselves and their accomplishments, and instead, spend many millions denigrating their opponents.

We have all heard or said to someone, "Stop acting like a baby." By that we don't mean to stop drinking out of a bottle or wearing diapers. Rather, we're talking about a person's infantile behavior—throwing tantrums and refusing to be reasonable when they don't get their way. Doesn't that sound like many of the adults in our day? The Lord says that "when He arises to shake the earth mightily" (Isaiah 2:19), He will give mankind "children to be their princes, and babes shall rule over them" (Isaiah 3:4). He will give whiny, tantrum-throwing, childish adults to lead people. Are we there yet?

In contrast, after God has completed the pouring out of His wrath during the tribulation and we are living in the millennium, and glorified saints are ruling with Jesus, who is sitting on the throne of David, the world will be different. For 1,000 years, there will be no childish behavior from leaders, and no unrighteous or unfair judgments. We will experience 1,000 years with no election years, no wasted money, no favoritism, no racism, no poverty, no unscientific mandates, etc. But when Satan is released at the end of Christ's 1,000-year kingdom, man's heart will be revealed for what it truly is: deceitfully wicked. And billions of people will side with Satan, rebelling against the one who treated them justly and fairly for 1,000 years.

If you are thinking, *You said everyone who enters the millennium is a believer*, that is correct. But not all the believers in the millennial kingdom will have glorified bodies. Isaiah 65:20 tells us, "No more shall an infant from there live but a few days, nor an old man who has not fulfilled his days; for the child shall die one hundred years old, but the sinner being one hundred years old shall be accursed."

The unglorified humans who entered the millennium as mortal human beings will be able to have children, and those children will go on to have children, and so on. All of these unglorified people will enjoy the Eden-like environment on earth. But they will be born sinners, just as we are today, and therefore, death will be a reality during the millennium, just as it was in Noah's day, even though people lived for hundreds of years. And there will be many who persist in their sin, which is foolish:

> Why do the nations rage,
> and the people plot a vain thing?
> The kings of the earth set themselves,
> and the rulers take counsel together,
> against the LORD and against His Anointed, saying,
> "Let us break their bonds in pieces
> and cast away Their cords from us."
>
> He who sits in the heavens shall laugh;
> the LORD shall hold them in derision.
> Then He shall speak to them in His wrath,
> and distress them in His deep displeasure:
> "Yet I have set My King
> on My holy hill of Zion."
>
> "I will declare the decree:
> The LORD has said to Me,
> 'You are My Son,
> today I have begotten You.
> Ask of Me, and I will give You
> the nations for Your inheritance,

and the ends of the earth for Your possession.
You shall break them with a rod of iron;
You shall dash them to pieces like a potter's vessel.'"

PSALM 2:1-9

Satan is not stupid, but he is a fool to think any number of humans could possibly overthrow the beloved city and destroy its King. Without question, this will be the biggest battle in history attempted by the biggest army in history. But it will also be the shortest battle in history. The Lord will call down fire from heaven, and His enemies will be consumed instantly by the fire.

This final rebellion against God will take place at the end of the millennium—a time during which God will prove how much He loves mankind and wants to save people. First, He sent His Son to die for the sins of the whole world, and the gift of salvation is available to anyone who desires it. Then God will follow up by having His Son rule the earth fairly and equitably for an entire millennium. Yet when Satan is released for a short time at the end of the millennium, billions will side with him and surround the camp of the saints and the beloved city of Jerusalem in a rebellion against the Lord and His anointed.

Again, this will be the largest war in history, as well as the shortest. No other war has numbered its combatants in numbers "as the sand of the sea" (Revelation 20:8), and no other battle of any magnitude was over before it even began. The nations will gather from the four corners of the earth and surround the beloved city of the saints, and before a single shot is fired, God will win with fire from heaven.

As we see the Lord's response to the gathering of the nations against Him, we are reminded of Psalm 103:9: "He will not always strive with us, nor will He keep His anger forever." What happens after this becomes much more understandable in light of all that God has done to get man to choose Him over the devil, which is the great white throne judgment.

The sad truth is that there are some things that only divine judgment can bring to an end. No matter what God does, when man is left on his own, he always winds up in the same place: in sin and rebellion against God. It doesn't matter whether God gives mankind one command, ten commands, or even 613 rules to observe to make life better and preserve their identity as God's special ones. And even when God pays the full redemptive price for people's sins through the blood of His own Son, in the end, most of mankind will still choose Satan and sin.

No matter what God does, when man is left
on his own, he always winds up in the same
place: in sin and rebellion against God.

In Revelation 20:7-8, we read the sad statement that "Satan will be released from his prison and will go out to deceive the nations which are in the four corners of the earth…to gather them for battle." We are not told how long this will take, but the compact nature of the record here seems to indicate it will happen quickly. Which means that people's hearts will have already turned against God even before Satan is released. This will be true even after the world has been at its best for 1,000 years. Conditions will be like they were in Eden, life spans will be long, people will enjoy good health, there will be no political corruption and no unfair punishment. Though it will be God who makes all this possible, people will still side with Satan anyway.

By this time, the long-suffering patience of the Lord will have reached its end. He will have done all He can to bring people to salvation, yet He will still be despised and rejected by men. Next will come the great white throne judgment.

CHAPTER 12

FROM HERE TO ETERNITY

W e now come to what can only be described as the most chilling scene in all the Bible. There is one verse in the midst of Revelation chapters 21–22 that I have long felt to be the most sobering set of words ever strung together to form a sentence:

> He who is unjust, let him be unjust still; he who is filthy, let him be filthy still; he who is righteous, let him be righteous still; he who is holy, let him be holy still.
>
> **REVELATION 22:11**

The permanence of people's final state is what makes this verse so sobering. The unjust and the filthy will remain unjust and filthy forever. The righteous and holy will stay righteous and holy forever. The contrast here is stunning, as is the overall theme of the end of Revelation 20 and the last two chapters of Scripture.

The Bible often uses contrast to highlight the distinction between living for God and living apart from God. One of the most vivid illustrations of this is found in Psalm 1, where we read of the contrast between the life experience of a righteous person and an unrighteous one.

The person who "walks not in the counsel of the ungodly, nor stands in the path of sinners, nor sits in the seat of the scornful" is "like a tree planted by the rivers of water" (verses 1, 3). The text says, in contrast, that "the ungodly are not so, but are like the chaff which the wind drives away. Therefore the ungodly shall not stand in the judgment." The word translated "stand" means "to endure."

Revelation 21–22 is formatted in much the same way. The New Jerusalem is described in all its majestic beauty, and the city is likened to a bride on her wedding day. In contrast, Revelation 21:8 then says, "But the cowardly, unbelieving, abominable, murderers, sexually immoral, sorcerers, idolaters, and all liars shall have their part in the lake which burns with fire and brimstone, which is the second death."

Later in Revelation 21, we find the same pattern:

> I saw no temple in it, for the Lord God Almighty and the Lamb are its temple. The city had no need of the sun or of the moon to shine in it, for the glory of God illuminated it. The Lamb is its light. And the nations of those who are saved shall walk in its light, and the kings of the earth bring their glory and honor into it. Its gates shall not be shut at all by day (there shall be no night there). And they shall bring the glory and the honor of the nations into it. But there shall by no means enter it anything that defiles, or causes an abomination or a lie, but only those who are written in the Lamb's Book of Life.
>
> **REVELATION 21:22-27**

Then one last time, in the final chapter of the Bible, we find yet another contrast:

> Blessed are those who do His commandments, that they may have the right to the tree of life, and may enter through

the gates into the city. But outside are dogs and sorcerers and sexually immoral and murderers and idolaters, and whoever loves and practices a lie.

REVELATION 22:14-15

Some people have asked if this means that people in hell will be able to see us in heaven, or if there will be unbelievers lurking outside of the celestial city. The Greek word translated "outside" is used to describe unbelievers in 1 Corinthians 5:12-13: "What have I to do with judging those also who are outside? Do you not judge those who are inside? But those who are outside God judges. Therefore 'put away from yourselves the evil person.'"

The contrasts we just read reveal that there are two eternal destinies. Contrary to what universalists teach, not everyone will end up in heaven because God is love. The contrasts in Scripture cannot be read any other way—they are not figurative. The New Jerusalem will be the eternal home of all believers, and the lake of fire will be the eternal home of all unbelievers. Every person ever born will end up in one of two eternal destinations, and that destination will be determined by the presence or absence of that person's name in the Lamb's Book of Life: "He who overcomes shall be clothed in white garments, and I will not blot out his name from the Book of Life; but I will confess his name before My Father and before His angels" (Revelation 3:5).

Every person ever born will end up in one of two eternal destinations, and that destination will be determined by the presence or absence of that person's name in the Lamb's Book of Life.

There has been substantial debate over whether names can be blotted out of the Book of Life. Some see Revelation 3:5 as proof that a Christian can lose their salvation, which would make Jesus' statement a threat and not a promise. Others say this means that everyone has their name written in the Book of Life, and unbelief blots it out. That is beyond unlikely, for that would imply everyone is saved at birth, and they lose their salvation later through unbelief.

It is my belief that what Jesus said is consistent with other statements He made about us: No one can snatch us from the Father's hand (John 10:29), and nothing can separate us from His love (Romans 8:38-39). Revelation 3:5 is not a threat, but a promise. That raises the question: How do you get your name written in the Book of Life, never to be blotted out?

Let's start by looking at the encounter between Jesus and Nicodemus:

> There was a man of the Pharisees named Nicodemus, a ruler of the Jews. This man came to Jesus by night and said to Him, "Rabbi, we know that You are a teacher come from God; for no one can do these signs that You do unless God is with him." Jesus answered and said to him, "Most assuredly, I say to you, unless one is born again, he cannot see the kingdom of God."
>
> JOHN 3:1-3

Everyone who is born again is written in the Book of Life!

We are given more details in the book of Revelation:

> I saw a great white throne and Him who sat on it, from whose face the earth and the heaven fled away. And there was found no place for them. And I saw the dead, small and great, standing before God, and books were opened. And another book was opened, which is the Book of Life.

And the dead were judged according to their works, by the things which were written in the books. The sea gave up the dead who were in it, and Death and Hades delivered up the dead who were in them. And they were judged, each one according to his works. Then Death and Hades were cast into the lake of fire. This is the second death. And anyone not found written in the Book of Life was cast into the lake of fire.

REVELATION 20:11-15

Hades is the temporary habitation of the souls of the unbelieving dead. Death refers to the grave that holds their bodies. Like believers, who will experience a bodily resurrection at the rapture, unbelievers will be bodily resurrected and their bodies will be reunited with their souls at the end of the millennium. However, it will not be a resurrection to the same destination as believers. Instead, unbelievers will find themselves standing before the throne of Almighty God, and books will be opened that record all their deeds, including all the times they rejected God's offer of salvation.

This group will include all who denied God as creator, all who followed false religions, all idolaters who worshipped other gods, all who believed that being a good moral person gains a person entrance into heaven and, as we read earlier in Revelation 21:8, "the cowardly, unbelieving, abominable, murderers, sexually immoral, sorcerers, idolaters, and all liars shall have their part in the lake which burns with fire and brimstone, which is the second death."

Before we move on, I need to make one point clear: There will be people in heaven who once did the things described above. There's an important distinction we need to understand with regard to those who go to heaven and those who go to hell:

> The works of the flesh are evident, which are: adultery, fornication, uncleanness, lewdness, idolatry, sorcery, hatred, contentions, jealousies, outbursts of wrath, selfish ambitions, dissensions, heresies, envy, murders, drunkenness, revelries, and the like; of which I tell you beforehand, just as I also told you in time past, that those who practice such things will not inherit the kingdom of God.
>
> GALATIANS 5:19-21

It is the *unrepentant* and *habitual* practice of those things that is the distinguishing factor between the people who are resurrected to heaven or to hell. First John 1:9 tells us more: "If we confess our sins, He is faithful and just to forgive us our sins and to cleanse us from all unrighteousness."

The word "confess" means "to see as the same," or "to speak of as the same." In other words, if we see sin as what God says it is, and we agree with God's definition of sin, He is faithful and just to forgive our sins and cleanse us from all unrighteousness.

In 1 John 2:4, we read, "He who says, 'I know Him,' and does not keep His commandments, is a liar, and the truth is not in him." Later in 1 John, we read,

> Little children, let no one deceive you. He who practices righteousness is righteous, just as He is righteous. He who sins is of the devil, for the devil has sinned from the beginning. For this purpose the Son of God was manifested, that He might destroy the works of the devil. Whoever has been born of God does not sin, for His seed remains in him; and he cannot sin, because he has been born of God.
>
> 1 JOHN 3:7-9

The Greek phrase translated "does not sin" is not implying sinless perfection is possible in this life. Rather, the phrase means "not content to continue." In other words, born-again Christians—who were all born as sinners—are not content to continue in sin after true regeneration. This answers the age-old question, How can you know you are saved? If you are content with your old way of life, and you have no desire to change in order to live for Christ and represent Him through your actions and words, then that doesn't reflect the presence of the Holy Spirit in your life.

When we become new creations we are no longer to live as we used to. Second Corinthians 5:17 says, "If anyone is in Christ, he is a new creation; old things have passed away; behold, all things have become new." This truth is not presented here as a directive, but rather, a reality. When you come to Christ, you become someone new. Your past record of all wrongdoings is wiped away, and *all* things—including your passions and desires—become new. The works of the flesh mentioned in Galatians 5:19-21 will no longer define your desires. This is the distinguishing factor between those who take part in the two resurrections and their distinct eternal destinies. Christians have sinned and will sin, but they don't defend it, try to redefine it, or try to find a loophole to allow what God has forbidden. The Holy Spirit in them is grieved, and so are they. They lose their contentment when in sin.

The contrast is that the unregenerate person who may have raised a hand or walked down an aisle or even prayed a sinner's prayer yet remains the same person they were before they did any of those things has not had old things pass away and all things become new. This is not to say that after we are born again we do everything we should and never do anything we shouldn't. It simply means a new path has been established and life begins to look different than it used to. For some people, the transformation may be highly noticeable because of the nature of their past practices. For others, the changes may not be as visible, but there is no question that, in big and small ways, knowing Christ has changed them.

When we are born again, the Lord begins to work on us and in us so He can work through us. He will do this until the day we go home through the rapture or death. As Philippians 1:6 says, "He who has begun a good work in you will complete it until the day of Jesus Christ."

> When we are born again, the Lord begins to work
> on us and in us so He can work through us.

Some people change dramatically and rapidly, others more subtly and gradually. Desires and passions will change, and priorities will change too. I have seen literally tens of thousands of people make commitments to Christ, and the most consistent way to sort out which commitments were real and which weren't is how a person goes on to treat the Word and church. True converts don't have a one-and-done approach to what happened the day they made a commitment to Christ. They persist in their hunger and thirst for righteousness. They want to learn God's Word and be around God's people, and the sins that used to be pleasurable to them have lost their appeal.

You may have noticed a heavier concentration of Scripture passages in this chapter than in the others. The reason is the truths in this chapter don't allow for other interpretations. Remember the "unjust still" and "holy still" passage we looked at earlier. This is what we are talking about: going from here to eternity. This chapter also addresses the most important of all issues regarding humanity as a whole, and answers one of the proverbial "big questions" of life: What happens after you die? The answer, according to the infallible Word of God, is that we will all go to an eternal destiny. Some will go to heaven, and others will go to hell. Every person has a final destination. There are no after-death opportunities for purification or times of penance in the hopes of changing that destiny.

As Hebrews 9:27 says, "It is appointed for men to die once, but after this the judgment." There no such place or purpose called purgatory. The Bible makes it quite clear that there is one decision in life that determines the address of your eternal destiny, and that is to be for or against Jesus Christ. To state that there is a place in the afterlife where we can become purified so that we can enter heaven is to deny the sufficiency of the blood of Jesus to cleanse us from all sin. You cannot pay your way into or out of an eternal destiny. Acts of penance cannot cover sin, and repeating certain phrases cannot cleanse you from all unrighteousness. To have your name written in the Lamb's Book of Life, you must be born again.

In our day, it is especially important that we remember that Jesus is presented to us in John chapter 1 as "the Word." That means you cannot accept Christ as Savior and reject portions of His Word. It's a package deal, and the two cannot be separated. Yet today, many have decided that a cut-and-paste approach to the Word of God is acceptable to Him. Those who are of that mindset need to consider the words of King David in Psalm 138:2: "I will worship toward Your holy temple, and praise Your name for Your lovingkindness and Your truth; for You have magnified Your word above all Your name."

The Lord Himself esteems His Word above His name, and many today are perfectly comfortable with doing the opposite, exalting their name above His Word. In other words, to reject portions of God's Word is to put your name above His. That would include justifications like "Man wrote the Bible," or "The Bible has been translated too many times to still be accurate," or "The moral precepts given in Scripture were relevant only at the time of its writing."

These are dangerous positions to hold about the Bible and could very well land those who hold them at the great white throne judgment.

For anyone who is thinking, *Wait a minute—we're saved by grace, not works,* remember this: Believing that God's Word is inspired and authoritative is not works, it's faith. And as Hebrews 11:6 says, "Without faith it is impossible to please Him, for he who comes to God must believe that He is, and that He is a rewarder of those who diligently seek Him."

As we close out this section of this chapter, I urge you to make sure you are born again. You don't want to take a chance when it comes to your eternal destiny. The moment that Jesus takes the church to be where He is will happen in the twinkling of an eye—faster than you can blink. And life is going to become unbelievably hard on earth.

In John 8:51, Jesus said, "Most assuredly, I say to you, if anyone keeps My word he shall never see death." It is the second death that is in view here (eternal condemnation) because of what we read in Hebrews 9:27 and Revelation 20:15: "It is appointed for men to die once, but after this the judgment," and "Anyone not found written in the Book of Life was cast into the lake of fire."

When it comes to our eternal destination, we must handle God's Word with great care. Second Timothy 3:16 declares, "All Scripture is given by inspiration of God, and is profitable for doctrine, for reproof, for correction, for instruction in righteousness."

The Holy Spirit is every bit as much God as the Father and Son are. The Spirit is the one who inspired all the words that humans wrote on the pages of the Bible. I cannot stress this enough: You can be wrong about the timing of the rapture, you can be wrong about the freewill or predestination debate, you can be wrong about whether Jesus was crucified on Thursday or Friday, and still be saved. But if you're wrong about the clear teachings of Scripture and you reject truths you don't like or agree with, then you are wrong in the most dangerous of all ways.

After the millennium will come the great white throne judgment for all unbelievers, none of whom have their names written in the Book of Life. In contrast, believers in Christ will see and experience this:

Now I saw a new heaven and a new earth, for the first heaven and the first earth had passed away. Also there was no more sea. Then I, John, saw the holy city, New Jerusalem, coming down out of heaven from God, prepared as a bride adorned for her husband. And I heard a loud voice from heaven saying, "Behold, the tabernacle of God is with men, and He will dwell with them, and they shall be His people. God Himself will be with them and be their God. And God will wipe away every tear from their eyes; there shall be no more death, nor sorrow, nor crying. There shall be no more pain, for the former things have passed away."

REVELATION 21:1-4

We will talk about the beauty and majesty of this city, which is compared to "a bride adorned for her husband," but first, let's address an issue that has troubled many believers throughout church history: How can heaven be heaven when people whom we loved, such as family members, went to hell?

I will not be dogmatic about this, but I do believe it is possible that what we just read in Revelation 21:1-4 gives us the answer. There are two popular opinions, and they are just that—opinions. One is that the wiping away of our tears is caused by the wiping away of our memories of those in hell. Because all the former things that caused pain will pass away, so will our memories of those who didn't end up in heaven. The other opinion is that the loss of loved ones to hell won't grieve us because we will be like Jesus (we will not be gods, but we will be perfect like Him), and consequently, we will see all things the way He does, including hell being a just and right punishment for those who rejected Him.

Whatever the answer happens to be, we can know that in heaven, we will know only joy and pleasure. Psalm 16:11 tells us, "You will show me the path of life; *in Your presence is fullness of joy; at Your right hand are pleasures forevermore.*" Can you imagine such an existence? Fullness and joy and pleasures forever! Come quickly, Lord Jesus!

I cannot do justice to the New Jerusalem by seeking to paraphrase or summarize what the Bible says about it. Read these words with anticipation and excitement, for they describe our eternal home:

> One of the seven angels who had the seven bowls filled with the seven last plagues came to me and talked with me, saying, "Come, I will show you the bride, the Lamb's wife." And he carried me away in the Spirit to a great and high mountain, and showed me the great city, the holy Jerusalem, descending out of heaven from God, having the glory of God. Her light was like a most precious stone, like a jasper stone, clear as crystal. Also she had a great and high wall with twelve gates, and twelve angels at the gates, and names written on them, which are the names of the twelve tribes of the children of Israel.
>
> REVELATION 21:9-12

> The construction of its wall was of jasper; and the city was pure gold, like clear glass. The foundations of the wall of the city were adorned with all kinds of precious stones: the first foundation was jasper, the second sapphire, the third chalcedony, the fourth emerald, the fifth sardonyx, the sixth sardius, the seventh chrysolite, the eighth beryl, the ninth topaz, the tenth chrysoprase, the eleventh jacinth, and the twelfth amethyst. The twelve gates were twelve pearls: each individual gate was of one pearl. And the street of the city was pure gold, like transparent glass.

> But I saw no temple in it, for the Lord God Almighty and the Lamb are its temple. The city had no need of the

sun or of the moon to shine in it, for the glory of God illuminated it. The Lamb is its light. And the nations of those who are saved shall walk in its light, and the kings of the earth bring their glory and honor into it. Its gates shall not be shut at all by day (there shall be no night there). And they shall bring the glory and the honor of the nations into it. But there shall by no means enter it anything that defiles, or causes an abomination or a lie, but only those who are written in the Lamb's Book of Life.

REVELATION 21:18-27

All of us have had things in this life that we have looked forward to. But the one thing we can look forward to above all others is not in this life, but the next: our eternal home. It will be special because of where we are, who we will be with, what it will be like, and what we will be able to do. We will live without sorrow or pain. Never again will we be tempted, or fail, or get sick. All we will know is joy and pleasure. We could keep going on and on, but the point is made.

Our eternal home...will be special because
of where we are, who we will be with, what it
will be like, and what we will be able to do.

Imagine a place where the glory of the Lord shines so brightly that there is no need for the sun—a place where there is no sun and yet no night. A place of absolute glory, where nothing that defiles or causes an abomination or a lie will ever enter. The New Jerusalem will have streets of purest gold, gates of single pearls, foundations of precious jewels, and best of all, the God and Father of our Lord Jesus Christ, and the Lord who paid our redemption price with His own blood.

I believe we are in the final phase of church history, and that we should live every day with the expectation that Jesus could rapture His church. I believe this because the preparations for the seventieth week of Daniel to be fulfilled began on May 14, 1948, when Israel became a nation once again.

I believe the end of all things is at hand because there has been a mass defection from truth within the church. Truth has been replaced with a form of godliness that denies the power of the gospel. I believe that most of what is called the church today has reached the Laodicean age, where people are the head of the church and not the Lord. There is, however, the true church, and it is but a remnant.

I believe that the tribulation is at the door because the perilous times Paul said would come have come. We are living in days like those of Noah. The earth is filled with violence, and the thoughts and intents of man's heart are only evil continually.

I believe we are in the last of the last days because the world is filled with incompetent, self-righteous, God-hating leaders who will do any-thing to hold on to power. Billions of people are looking for the gov-ernment to take care of them and are longing for a new world order.

I believe it is time for the church to go home because the com-batants of the Ezekiel war are assuming their positions and form-ing coalitions. The uniting and driving force behind the invasion, energy-related products, has come to the surface and is being used as a weapon like never before. To them, the golden rule says, "He who has the gold makes the rules." Therefore, he who controls the oil and gas markets rules. And the mechanisms and technology nec-essary to control the buying and selling activities of all humanity are already in place.

I believe that we are at the end of the time of the Gentiles and that we can see the day approaching. We know what to look for because the Lord saw fit to give us enough information to figure out when the day is drawing nearer. Everything He told us to watch for is happening in a birth pang-like progression. Deceivers who come in Jesus' name are all around us, wars and rumors of wars are escalating, ethnic tensions are rising, food and supply shortages are spreading, pestilences are now global, and geological and atmospheric anomalies have become the new normal. As Jesus said, "All these are the beginning of sorrows" (Matthew 24:8).

"Beginning of sorrows" could be translated "the commencement of labor pains." The precursors to the tribulation are all around us. I preached a message a few years ago in an effort to mark, as much as we can, where we are on the prophetic time line. Using Jesus' mention of the beginning of sorrows, I titled the message "The End of the Beginning." In other words, I believe the early labor pains portion of the prophetic progression is at its end, and the heavy labor pains of the tribulation are approaching quickly.

Jesus is coming soon, and we are to occupy till He comes. That means we need to be busy telling people about Jesus. Inviting people to church is good, provided you are inviting them to a Bible-teaching church. However, we are not commissioned to invite people to church. Rather, we are commissioned to tell people about Christ and invite them to be born again.

As we live in these perilous and delusional times, remember where we are going and who promised that destination. As we conclude this record of what we need to know about the time of the signs, it is fitting that we close with the last words of the greatest book ever written, the Word of God:

> Behold, I am coming quickly, and My reward is with
> Me, to give to every one according to his work. I am the
> Alpha and the Omega, the Beginning and the End, the
> First and the Last.

Blessed are those who do His commandments, that they may have the right to the tree of life, and may enter through the gates into the city. But outside are dogs and sorcerers and sexually immoral and murderers and idolaters, and whoever loves and practices a lie.

I, Jesus, have sent My angel to testify to you these things in the churches. I am the Root and the Offspring of David, the Bright and Morning Star.

And the Spirit and the bride say, "Come!" And let him who hears say, "Come!" And let him who thirsts come. Whoever desires, let him take the water of life freely.

For I testify to everyone who hears the words of the prophecy of this book: If anyone adds to these things, God will add to him the plagues that are written in this book; and if anyone takes away from the words of the book of this prophecy, God shall take away his part from the Book of Life, from the holy city, and from the things which are written in this book.

He who testifies to these things says, "Surely I am coming quickly."

Amen. Even so, come, Lord Jesus!

The grace of our Lord Jesus Christ be with you all. Amen.

REVELATION 22:12-21

NOTES

1. Vance Havner, *Pepper 'n Salt* (Old Tappan, NJ: Fleming H. Revell, 1966), page number unknown, see at https://library.melbac.org/books/vision/Pepper%20and%20Salt.pdf.

2. Mark Hitchcock, *Russia Rising* (Carol Stream, IL: Tyndale, 2017).

3. Cath Martin, "70 million Christians martyred for their faith since Jesus walked the earth," *Christianity Today*, June 25, 2014, https://www.christiantoday.com/article/70-million -christians-martyred-faith-since-jesus-walked-earth/38403.htm.

4. Dan Wooding, "Modern Persecution," *Christianity.com*, May 3, 2010, https://www.christianity .com/church/church-history/timeline/1901-2000/modern-persecution-11630665.html.

5. "Abortion leading cause of death around the world, killing more people than cancer and disease in 2022," *Society for the Protection of Unborn Children*, January 5, 2023, https.//www .spuc.org.uk/Article/385407/Abortion-leading-cause-of-death-around-the-world-killing-more -people-than-cancer-and-disease-in-2022.

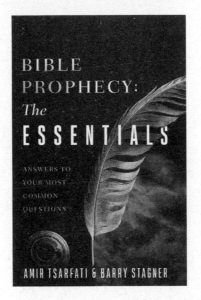

To learn more about our Harvest Prophecy resources, please visit:

www.HarvestProphecyHQ.com

HARVEST PROPHECY
AN IMPRINT OF HARVEST HOUSE PUBLISHERS